P9-BYJ-071

CASS LIBRARY OF AFRICAN STUDIES

TRAVELS AND NARRATIVES

No. 67

Editorial Adviser: JOHN RALPH WILLIS
Department of History, University of California, Berkeley

TRAVELS IN EASTERN AFRICA

AFRICAN TRAVELS AND NARRATIVES

No. 59. John M'Leod
A Voyage to Africa with Some Account of the Manners and Customs of the Dahomian People (1820).
New Impression

No. 60. Captain Hugh Crow
Memoirs of the late Captain Hugh Crow, of Liverpool, comprising a narrative of his life, together with descriptive sketches of the Western Coast of Africa; particularly of Bonny; . . . to which are added, anecdotes and observations, illustrative of the Negro character (1830).
New Impression

No. 61. James Richardson
Narrative of a Mission to Central Africa Performed in the Years 1850–1851 (1853).
New Impression

No. 62. James Richardson
Travels in the Great Desert of Sahara in the years of 1845 and 1846, . . . Including a Description of the Oases and Cities of Ghet Ghadames and Mourzuk (1848).
New Impression

No. 63. Thomas J. Hutchinson
Impressions of Western Africa with Remarks on the Diseases of the Climate and a Report on the Peculiarities of Trade up the Rivers in the Bight of Biafra (1858).
New Impression

No. 64. Joseph Hawkins
A History of a Voyage to the Coast of Africa, and Travels into the interior of that country, containing particular descriptions of the Climate and Inhabitants, and interesting particulars concerning the Slave Trade (1796; 2nd ed. 1797).
New Impression

No. 65. Henry Jules Blanc
A Narrative of Captivity in Abyssinia; with Some Account of the late Emperor Theodore, his Country and People (1868).
New Impression

No. 66. Filippo Pigafetta
A Report of the Kingdom of Congo, and of the Surrounding Countries; Drawn out of the Writings and Discourses of the Portuguese, Duarte Lopez (1591).
Translated from the Italian and edited with explanatory notes by Margarite Hutchinson (1881).
New Impression

No. 67. Lyons McLeod
Travels in Eastern Africa; with the Narrative of a residence in Mozambique (1860).
New Impression

TRAVELS

IN

EASTERN AFRICA;

WITH

The Narrative of a Residence in Mozambique

BY

LYONS McLEOD

IN TWO VOLUMES

VOLUME I

FRANK CASS & CO. LTD.

1971

Published by
FRANK CASS AND COMPANY LIMITED
67 Great Russell Street, London WC1B 3BT

First published 1860
New impression 1971

ISBN 0 7146 1832 2

Printed in Great Britain by Clarke, Doble & Brendon Ltd.
Plymouth and London

J Saddler.

LYONS Mc LEOD, F.R.G.S.

&c. &c.

London: Hurst & Blackett, 1860.

TRAVELS IN EASTERN AFRICA;

WITH

THE NARRATIVE OF A RESIDENCE IN MOZAMBIQUE.

BY

LYONS McLEOD, Esq., F.R.G.S.,

HONORARY FELLOW OF THE ROYAL SOCIETY OF ARTS AND SCIENCES
AND OF THE METEOROLOGICAL SOCIETY, MAURITIUS
LATE H.B.M. CONSUL AT MOZAMBIQUE.

THE ROYAL OBSERVATORY, CAPE OF GOOD HOPE.

Ethiopia shall soon stretch out her hands unto God."—*Psalm* LXVIII. *v.* 31.

IN TWO VOLUMES.

VOL. I.

LONDON:
HURST AND BLACKETT, PUBLISHERS,
SUCCESSORS TO HENRY COLBURN,
13, GREAT MARLBOROUGH STREET.
1860.

TO THE

MERCHANTS AND MEMBERS OF CHAMBERS OF COMMERCE OF GREAT BRITAIN AND IRELAND.

GENTLEMEN,

Impressed with the conviction that, from the most remote time, Civilization and Christianity have been best promoted by Commerce, which binds rival nations in the bonds of Peace, I respectfully dedicate this work to the Mercantile portion of my countrymen, in the hope that by their united efforts, Slavery may be made to disappear from the continent of Africa, through the establishment of commercial relations, especially with that rich portion of its coast and the neighbouring Ethiopian Archipelago, including the fertile island of Madagascar, described in the following pages.

I have the honor to be,

GENTLEMEN,

Your most obedient and humble Servant,

THE AUTHOR.

CONTENTS

OF

THE FIRST VOLUME.

CHAPTER I.

CHAPTER II.

CHAPTER III.

CHAPTER IV.

CHAPTER V.

CHAPTER VI.

CHAPTER VII.

CHAPTER VIII.

CHAPTER IX.

CHAPTER X.

CHAPTER XI.

TRAVELS IN EASTERN AFRICA.

CHAPTER I.

The "Ireland"—W.S.L. Postal-line—Mr. Jenkins—The Author Discovers that he is Styled a "Government"—The General's Quarters—Proceed to Sea—Accident in the Saloon—Total Darkness in the "Lower Regions"—Spittoons and Safety Lamps—The Gale—Put Back to Plymouth—Ten Passengers Leave the "Ireland."

On the 6th December, 1856, I embarked, with my wife, on board the Royal Mail Screw Steamer "Ireland," for the Cape of Good Hope, *en route* to Mozambique, to which place I had been appointed as Her Majesty's Consul.

Externally, the "Ireland" was what sailors call a very "tidy craft." She was about 1,000 tons burthen; long, low, and rakish; having three masts and one funnel, and what is called a stump bowsprit. As she was fitted with a screw propeller, she was devoid of those great protuberances called paddle-boxes, which in a steamer so materially (to my eye) destroy the symmetry of the hull of the vessel, which, in this case, was built of iron, and painted entirely black.

Flying at the mizen peak was the well known ensign of Old England, the field of which appeared to me unusually disfigured by the talismanic letters, W.S.L., in a glaring yellow colour, begrimed by soot.

On asking the meaning of those letters, I was told that they were the initials of an M.P., who had not only sufficient interest to obtain the contract for carrying the mail in a line of very slow steamers, but who was held in such dread by a venerable body of old gentlemen sitting behind the sign of the "Sea Horses," in Whitehall, known as the Board of Admiralty, that the M.P., W.S.L., was permitted to place the initials of his name on the national ensign, without being subjected to the usual fines and penalties inflicted on those similarly offending. Others told me that W.S.L. stood for the "worst steam line," but this I looked upon as the invention of some disappointed mail contractor.

Such was the "Ireland" externally; and, as she was at anchor in the beautiful little west-country harbour of Dartmouth, which boasted W.S.L. for its representative in the House of Commons, the saucy craft might well say, "I am monarch of all I survey."

Arriving alongside of the "Ireland," about one hour before her advertised time of sailing, in a small steamer full of fellow passengers, which had brought us some miles down the little river Dart, we imagined that there would be every accommodation for our reception; but, on the contrary, we found that we were not supposed to come near her for some imaginary time, which they on board could not name to us. All that we learned was, that the numerous barges then alongside of her, full of coals, had to be cleared of their cargoes before the passengers were allowed on board. To our repeated applications to be permitted alongside, we were told to return to the shore; and as it was raining very heavily, the man who was steering the small steamer, put her helm up and made for the land; however, this being done without the consent of the passengers, they soon took matters into their own hands, and compelled the small craft to dash alongside, causing considerable damage to the coal-barges. Exposed to a volley of abuse, some of the most adventurous of the gentlemen scrambled on board, and we were actually compelled to appeal to the commander of the vessel before we could get the ladies on the deck of the "Ireland."

It appears that we had unfortunately arrived alongside of the vessel at the cabin dinner-hour, and were exposed to all this inconvenience at the whim of the chief officer and the head steward; the former of whom wished to clear the coal-barges, and the latter to save himself the trouble of laying a few more plates on the table.

No sooner were we on board of this passenger ship than we found ourselves rudely pushed about, and, after having been driven round the wet deck with pigs, sheep, and poultry, with considerable difficulty we threaded our way through hampers, water-casks, coals, &c., to the cabin saloon.

This was an elegant apartment, decorated with gold and green, having at the further end a grate and marble mantel-piece; but as the chimney led to the screw propeller, of course, the first time a fire was lighted, the saloon and cabins were deserted in consequence of the smoke, which made one almost fancy that the ship was on fire; so it turned out to be for ornament and not for use.

Observing the state of confusion in which everything was on board this first-class passenger ship—being an old traveller—as soon as the ladies were placed in shelter from the rain, which was coming down in a most pitiless manner, I returned to the deck to look after my luggage, when I found that the chief officer had ordered the small steamer to return to the shore with the luggage of all those passengers who had succeeded in reaching the deck of the "Ireland," contrary to his wishes. This officer, who was promised a command in the W.S.L. Line of Steamers on his return to England, took upon himself to *mark* the passengers who had so offended him, and during the passage he had to be admonished by the commander for his marked rudeness to some of the ladies, as well as the gentlemen who had acted contrary to his wishes on the occasion referred to. On an application being made to the commander, the small steamer was ordered alongside, and we recovered our luggage.

Returning to the saloon, we found considerable commotion among the lady passengers, as it was discovered that the "ladies' saloon" had been appropriated for the use of a family.

To my inquiry for my cabin or state-room, the head steward replied, "You're a government passenger, sir—you must go below; your cabin is the aftermost one but one, on the starboard side of the lower deck. That's the way, sir! down that ladder." With considerable difficulty I descended a ladder which received many a blessing from the passengers during the voyage. Arrived at the bottom of the shaft (for I can liken the descent only to that into a coal mine), I found myself in a dark, dismal locality, always afterwards denominated the "lower regions." Here were squalling babies, fighting stewards, swearing sailors, and discontented everybodies.

On asking if there was any one there to point

out the cabins, a voice answered from a distance, "Why the d—l do you not come with that water? I will not get a bit of dinner this night;" while another one exclaimed, "I'll break your head if you do not hurry and bring me a light?" Even the children in this dismal place appeared to be bent on doing harm, and were engaged in combat with each other, or struggling with their weary and discontented nurses.

After making good use of my lungs, a queer-looking, red-headed, one-eyed individual, in shirt sleeves, made his appearance, carrying in his hand a tin spittoon, on the rim of which was the miserable remains of a purser's dip, by the flickering light of which I was examined from head to foot. Cautiously approaching, the stranger welcomed me on board, and requested me to make myself "quite at home."

To my inquiry, "Who are you?" he replied:— "It's all right, sir; you'll know me before long. On shore they call me 'Mr. Jenkins,' but on board this thing I am called the 'bed-room steward.' However, here we are for the voyage, sir, and we must make the best of it."

I asked "Mr. Jenkins" to show me my cabin, when he inquired what my name was. Having satisfied my interrogator on this point, he exclaimed:—

"Oh, you're a government; come this way, sir."

To my inquiry what he meant by calling me a "government," Mr. Jenkins replied, "You'll see directly, sir!"

Following this extraordinary being through a labyrinth of boxes, hampers, deal boards, carpenter's tools, and carpet-bags, we arrived at the door of a cabin, seizing the handle of which, Mr. Jenkins cautioned me not to be disappointed, and gently opened it. Being in the after part of the ship, I expected to find a small cabin, but not the miserable dog-hole now revealed to me. It was barely six feet in length, and its extreme breadth scarcely five feet.

To my exclamation that "there must be some mistake!" Mr. Jenkins replied:—

"No, sir; *he* never makes mistakes! You see, sir, you're a 'government,' as I told you before, and that is why *he* has given you this cabin."

After some exercise of patience and temper, I

learned from Mr. Jenkins that *he* meant W.S.L., and that the term a "government" applied to myself, referred to my being a government passenger, a certain number of whom are carried by all steamers belonging to lines which have a contract for carrying the mails.

To my observation that I was surprised that W.S.L. was not afraid to treat the government passengers in such a shameful manner, by putting them into cabins which he could not possibly let to any other passengers, Mr. Jenkins stated that "W.S.L. was not afraid of any government, that he hated all 'governments,' and when he got them on board of his ships he always served them in that way."

To this I could only remark, on more minutely examining the cabin, that it was a most disgraceful place to put a lady into. Jenkins, ever ready with an answer, immediately replied:—

"You see, sir, all 'governments' are supposed to be gentlemen—'governments' are not supposed to be married."

"But surely, Jenkins, there must be some better cabin than this still vacant?"

"No, sir, not one; take my advice and make the best of it. You see, sir, outside here in the steerage we have little enough room at any time, but, considering we are bound to a hot climate, it will be stifling in a fortnight's time—well, the Admiralty insist upon *his* taking the full number of 'governments' with him this voyage. Well, *he* has already let all the cabins and got paid for them; the consequence is that for one of 'the governments' *he* has ordered this 'structure' to be built. Just come and look at it, sir."

Following my loquacious friend, I managed at last to reach the hatchway close to which the carpenters were elevating what Jenkins had termed a "structure," to be adapted into a sleeping cabin for a gentleman, as I afterwards found, six feet in height.

Asking for an explanation of this stoppage to the ventilation of the "lower regions," Jenkins, ever ready to explain his part of this passenger ship, exclaimed:—

"This, sir, is what I wish particularly to point out to you; the men employed upon it call it the 'general's quarters,' the children call it 'Punch's house,' and I call it the 'structure.' Have you any interest, sir, with the Board of Trade?"

"What makes you ask such a question?"

"Don't be offended, sir; I have put that question to every 'government' that has come on board of this ship."

"If I was a 'government,' I would stop this ship—that 'structure' is sure to cause fever and death."

Leaving Mr. Jenkins gazing on the "structure," I hurried on deck and found my way into the saloon, where I explained the state of things below to my wife. I found that some ladies who had preceded us in their arrival on board, and who, like us, were government passengers, had already made her acquainted with the very inferior accommodation to which we were condemned for the voyage.

The ladies retired early that evening, for the greater number of them had travelled a considerable distance during the day; but what with the hammering kept up all night by the carpenters, the straw pillows, and the miserable coffins of berths, on comparing notes the next morning, it was found that but few among the passengers, male or female, slept during the first night on board the "Ireland."

On examining the "structure" the next morning, we perceived that it had visibly increased its dimensions during the night, thereby excluding light and air. Jenkins talked in a despairing tone of the "Board of Trade," and occasionally alluded to the "Emigration Commissioners," but despite this the "structure," accompanied by, if possible, increasing noise, progressed, greatly to the amusement of the little boys, and to the annoyance of all adults.

After breakfast we were told that the vessel would not be ready for sea before two days, and some of the passengers and myself went on shore in search of carpenters to fit up our cabins. In my cabin, the dimensions of which I have already given, there were two sleeping berths, the lower of which it was impossible for one to lie in, much less to sleep there; and this vessel was going to cross the equator twice during her outward voyage.

Such meagre accommodation would not have

been permitted in an emigrant vessel; and here was a mail steamer, under the pretence of being a first-class ship, obtaining passengers from the old established Indian traders, who were paying higher passage money than by those ships, and sixty passengers were crowded into a space where there was barely accommodation for half that number.

With the aid of a carpenter from the shore, the upper berth was enlarged, but with the lower one it was found impossible to do anything without curtailing the already small standing room. It was therefore turned into a receptacle for carpet-bags, and I made my mind up to sleep on the floor for the passage to the Cape of Good Hope.

With an outlay of about three pounds sterling on our *state-room*, it was made tenantable; and it was calculated that the passengers had expended about one hundred pounds on fittings in their cabins, or state-rooms, which ought to have been there on their arrival on board the "Ireland."

Evening came, and there was no cessation to the hammering which had been going on ever since we scrambled on board. The carpenters were to be employed another night in completing the "general's quarters," or, as the children would insist upon calling it, "Punch's house." It was therefore determined, by those whose unfortunate lot it was to have their state-rooms in the "lower regions," to remain in the saloon all night, as it was quite impossible to sleep with the hammering and shouting carried on below, accompanied, as it would be, by the thrilling tones of the interesting little darlings who had hitherto displayed very bellicose dispositions.

About eleven o'clock, we asked the head steward to furnish us with some supper; firstly, because we were really hungry; and, secondly, because we were all good-humouredly putting up with the great inconvenience of remaining in the saloon, instead of retiring to our cabins, we thought, and very naturally too, that some supper would have enabled us to pass the time more agreeably.

The steward appeared quite bewildered at our asking such a thing, and replied "that suppers were not allowed." But we were not to be put off with this reply. The passengers whose state-rooms led out of the saloon determined that their friends belonging to the "lower regions" should have some refreshments, and soon produced from their state-rooms innumerable delicacies, which had been laid in for the voyage. While enjoying this pic-nic, the unhappy steward, who foresaw in this demonstration the future violation of the rules and regulations of the W.S.L. Line of Steamers, without a moment's notice, put the lights out, and left us in utter darkness. Some of the young folks proposed a serenade, to which all willingly gave their consent, and in this agreeable manner another hour was passed.

At midnight the steward again made his appearance, and informed us that we were too noisy, and that we must disperse.

Under these circumstances, there was nothing to be done but to go below. Bidding our hospitable friends in the saloon state-rooms "pleasant dreams and sweet repose," we descended the ladder leading to the "lower regions," and formed ourselves into a committee of inspection on the "general's quarters," where we found a young indigo planter, of five years of age, was in possession of the premises, where he insisted upon rehearsing, even at that early hour, certain portions of Punch, much to the amusement of the carpenters working at the expense of W.S.L., and of some young Scotch cadets bound to India, who, even at that early period of the voyage, began to look upon young Frank Indigo as a "fearfu' laddie."

The whole of that night there was a continuation of hammering, shouting, singing, whistling, and crying. And thus another sleepless night was passed; and we were all glad when daylight dawned, and we repaired to the steamer's dirty deck.

On the afternoon of the 8th, preparations were made for going to sea; and about 5 P.M., Captain Bully, the agent of the W.S.L. Line of Steamers, came on board, and informed the commander of the "Ireland" that he must proceed to sea at once.

The steam was up, and, although thick clouds were seen banking up in the south west, the scud flying fast to the north east over our heads, the sea-birds, with their alarming cries, flying inland, and the mercury in the barometer falling rapidly, Captain Bully said these indications were "all nonsense," and that we would have fine weather; besides, if the mails were detained any longer, W.S.L. would be fined; and that therefore we must go to sea, after which he had nothing to do with us. Accordingly, at 6 P.M., we passed from the snug little harbour of Dartmouth into the English Channel, to breast a gale of whose approach even the ducks and geese on board the ship were sensible.

As soon as we got into the Channel, we found it was blowing fresh, with a heavy cross sea from the south west. The engines were weak, and, although the screw propeller made a great deal of noise, it did very little work.

In two hours' time all the passengers were obliged to retire to their state-rooms, with the exception of a few old tars, myself being numbered among the latter.

As the night advanced the wind grew louder, the sea more boisterous, and the straining and creaking of the ship, together with those mysterious noises which are heard in a new vessel, increased.

In the "lower regions" we were entirely in darkness, and it appeared impossible to procure a light in the state-rooms.

In the middle of this melancholy state of affairs, a fearful crash was heard in the saloon, which conveyed the impression to those below that something serious had happened. The report was immediately circulated in the "lower regions" that the marble mantel-piece had been carried away, killing three of the gentlemen in the saloon. When the accident occurred, I happened to be in the saloon, and was fortunate in saving one gentleman from seriously injuring himself. The fact was that the seats or benches running along the saloon-tables were secured to the deck by large screws, which, being made of inferior metal, or imperfectly cast, snapped off during one of the heavy rolls of the vessel; the consequence was that all those persons seated on the bench which gave way were precipitated with some considerable violence against the side cabins, suffering more or less injury. The second officer and two of the passengers were a good deal hurt, the officer being carried to his cabin.

As I sat at the end of the table, near the marble mantel-piece, until the real circumstances of the case were known, it was supposed by many that I was one of those injured, and, on descending to the "lower regions," I found my wife, who is a great sufferer at sea, almost dead with terror. For, it appears, she heard those outside of her cabin say that three of the gentlemen were killed. This accident had such an effect upon her nervous system, that she did not recover from it for the whole voyage.

On asking Mr. Jenkins the cause of his portion of the ship being in darkness, he replied that "the candles sent on board were too large for the lamps in the state-rooms, and that it was impossible for one man to cut them down fast enough."

Jenkins had no one to help him, his ordinary assistants having to yield to the "*mal de mer*," and he was at his wit's end what to do to keep the place lighted. Fertile in invention, on this occasion a most amusing idea came to his aid. In the earlier part of the day he had come across some dozens of tin spittoons, which had been sent on board the vessel, by a mistake, for some other articles of more importance. Jenkins bethought him of these useless implements, and having tried one of the offending candles, he found that it would just fit into the spittoon, and he at once decided upon saving himself the trouble of reducing the candles by placing them in the spittoons. Accordingly, on a bed-room candle-stick being asked for, Jenkins handed one of these spittoons, with a candle in it, accompanied by a polite bow and a bland smile, as if he was supplying the latest fashion of safety-lamp. It was afterwards suggested to Jenkins, by a lady, that if the candles were held in hot water they might be evenly reduced to any diameter; while, at the same time, there would be a considerable saving of the material, which Jenkins might turn into money on getting into harbour. The hint was taken, and the passengers were not compelled to use a spittoon for a bed-cabin candle-stick.

There was little sleep in the "Ireland" that

night, what with the noise below, the rolling and pitching of the ship, the screams of the affrighted children, the rushing of feet upon deck, the noise of the steam, and the screw-propeller—all occasionally hushed in the howling of the tempest. Still the "Ireland" had to breast the sea, and it would be no common gale that would induce her determined commander to put back.

About four o'clock the next morning, we were disturbed by a noise which made every one in the afterpart of the vessel, below the upper deck, imagine, for a moment, that the ship had struck a rock, so violent was the shock given to the frame of the vessel.

On inquiry, it was ascertained that one of the extra water-tanks carried on deck, not having been lashed, had got adrift; and, after having first nearly unshipped the funnel, it brought up against the bulwark, where it injured the side of the vessel considerably.

So slight a cause creating so violent a shock gave us but a poor opinion of the frame of the ship, which we found was built by contract.

The storm continued with that loud howling of the wind, and sharp whistling among the shrouds, which betokened the increase of the gale; while, occasionally, the vessel would descend into the sea as if she were overburdened, and anon a mighty sea would strike, arresting her in her progress, and making her shake from stem to stern.

At five o'clock the close-reefed topsails were blown into ribbons, the storm staysail was torn to shreds, and the engines, unassisted by canvas, soon gave indications of their weakness. It was found that the machinery was totally unfit to drive the vessel in the face of the gale and sea with which she had to contend. As day dawned, there was every prospect of an increase of the gale, and the prudent commander determined to seek shelter while yet the engines were not disabled. Hardly had we bore up for Plymouth, when the gale increased, and, by the rapid falling of the barometer, we had reasons for believing that the most dangerous part of the revolving storm passed very near to us.

As soon as we were at anchor under shelter in

the magnificent breakwater at Plymouth, the passengers began to make their appearance in the saloon, and it was then discovered that there were not seats for many of them at the table; in consequence of which, and the general discontent at the arrangements on board, ten of the passengers left the ship.

This created some vacancies in the state-rooms leading out of the saloon, and as I was obliged to go on by that mail, I insisted upon having one of the vacant state-rooms, by which means we left the "lower regions." All the fixtures which we had put up for our comfort were removed to our new quarters, and the ladies on board said that my wife's cabin was the most comfortable in the vessel, which I thought was not saying much for it.

During our late cruise, many of the ladies who had embarked without their husbands fared very badly. Mrs. R., with two children and a nurse, passengers to Mauritius, from the hour she came on board, on the eve of our departure from Dartmouth, until her husband stepped on deck at Plymouth, to take herself and little ones on shore, had not tasted anything with the exception of a little cold water taken from a can in her cabin, which was so strong of paint that it made herself and her children quite ill. Of course this lady and her family did not return to the "Ireland" after landing at Plymouth, nor would any of her friends sail again in any vessel having W.S.L. connected with her.

Soon after our arrival at Plymouth, we had a warm invitation from our friends on shore to renew our late visit. We got a good ducking while reaching the shore in one of the Plymouth boats; but this and our past dangers were soon forgotten in the affectionate greetings and smiling welcomes of our kind friends. But this was not to last long, for the next day, as we were sitting down to an early Sunday dinner, a carriage drove up to the door, with a note from the Captain of the "Ireland," telling us that he was going to start immediately; so, once more taking a hasty farewell of our hospitable friends, we found ourselves again on board the "Ireland."

CHAPTER II.

Departure from Plymouth—Reflections on Leaving England—Cabin Attendants—Live Stock—Mr. Jenkins and "the Pure Element"—N.E. Trades—Red Atlantic Dust—Short Allowance of Water—Viewing the "Line"—The Southern Cross—A Lady Navigator—"Fire! Fire!"—The Maniac—Arrival at the Cape.

It was a beautiful Sunday evening when we again embarked in the "Ireland." The gale had been succeeded by a calm which lent enchantment to the view of the rich and varied scenery of Plymouth harbour. Evening was closing in, and anon from the shore might be heard the bells of the churches and chapels calling on man to praise his Maker.

The steam was up, the passengers were all embarked, the latest mail-bags had just arrived, so that the "Ireland" once more moved into the

English Channel. This time the "Channel of Old England" was as still as a mill-pond, and mirrored the bright stars of the firmament as the busy steamers glided about with their red and green lights, warning each other of danger.

Many an eye was cast on the receding shores of that loved island, never to gaze upon it more. Many sad hearts were sighing for homes never to be visited again.

Of the numerous passengers pacing that deck, and thinking of those who would miss them at the accustomed hearths, as the long winter evenings set in, how few were destined to return to the homes they loved so well!

Some of the brave men who talked so lightly then, and tried to cheer the drooping spirits of their fair companions, were to be sorely tried in a distant clime, and to fall gloriously struggling to retain India for the land of their birth.

Wives going to their longing husbands were destined never to meet them—or only in danger and in death.

Longing hearts were then on the way to be wedded to those whose plight had been trothed many years before, and now, having earned independence, invited their young loves to share it.

Girls blooming into womanhood, bound for their unknown journey in the East, were soon to find rest in death.

The majority of the passengers were journeying to India, then on the eve of rebellion. Loving wife, gallant soldier, blooming maiden, and almost lisping childhood, were destined to take their part in that awful tragedy, the acts of which may never be told.

Not one-fourth part of the passengers in the "Ireland" on that voyage are now living; and even of the survivors, some have been sorely tried, as the pages of this book will reveal. But I must not anticipate.

I have travelled much, but I have never met with a party of ladies who had such a strong presentiment of coming evil. Many and many a time have some of those, who are now no more, expressed their dread, not only of proceeding in the vessel, but even of going to India; although they were then on the way to those they loved best on earth.

In a few days we had all shaken into our places, and, despite sundry inconveniences, we were determined to be happy, and that goes a long way in this world, both on shore and afloat, to render unhappy mortals as we are contented with our lot.

It is true that the stewardess, being too fond of the "cratur" in her coffee, the ladies dispensed with her services as much as possible; and that the servants being altogether inadequate in number for the work which they had to perform, the greater part of the attendance at table fell upon the gentlemen passengers, who, to stop the daily occurrence of the soup being poured over the ladies, kindly offered their services during dinner time.

These cabin assistants, or incumbrances, eventually drove the head steward out of his mind. On going to sea, the poor man found that the cabin-servants had never been in a vessel before, having shipped on board for the purpose of learning their duty, with which understanding they were paid accordingly, at the rate of ten shillings per month, and to pay for their own breakages.

The balance these men would have to receive on the pay-day would indeed be very trifling, for they were always breaking. One poor youth, who had not got his "sea legs," fell down and broke thirteen dishes at once, and as for plates, they appeared to be broken by dozens.

The live stock placed on board at Dartmouth was the admiration of every one; and yet, from there not being one man expressly to look after the stock, fowls, ducks, and geese disappeared very quickly, literally dying in the coops from starvation and want of water. At last the gentlemen passengers, as a matter of precaution, made a point of examining the stock every morning, in order that they might see those thrown overboard which had died during the previous night.

On one occasion I recollect seeing eleven dead geese thrown overboard; and from this neglect a vessel that was most liberally found, on starting from England, for the entire voyage to India, ran short of everything before she arrived at the Cape of Good Hope.

The ladies were without a bath during the whole voyage, although there was a comfortable bath-room on board; owing to the pump not being properly fitted, the bath could only be filled once a day, during the time of washing the decks before breakfast. To overcome this difficulty, the stewardess very coolly proposed that a certain number of the ladies should bathe in the same water each day; a proposition which of course found no seconder in those most interested, and in consequence only one lady could enjoy the luxury of a bath per diem.

It was found that 2,000 gallons of fresh water had been destroyed, by letting the salt water run into the tank while washing decks. This water, being impossible to drink, was set aside for washing water, to be used in the cabins. Jenkins thought that pure salt water was equally as good for washing the body, and therefore supplied the cabins with the "pure element," while he disposed of that which was brackish to those who were glad to pay him for the same.

Soon after we had entered the North East Trade Wind, and more especially when passing the Cape de Verde Islands, the atmosphere assumed that hazy appearance so remarkable during the blowing of the Harmattan winds on the west coast of Africa. But on the present occasion I did not experience that dryness of the air of which one is made so sensible during a Harmattan wind. When at the river Gambia, some years previous, the feeling caused by the dryness of the Harmattan wind was, although generally pleasant and very bracing, at times painful; the skin being dried up and wrinkled, and a general feeling, on the surface of the body, as if suffering from an attack of acute rheumatism. The teeth were affected as if one had been using some very strong acid in the mouth, and the bones of the head and face were slightly painful; and yet I am inclined to think that these were not rheumatic affections.

During the prevalence of these winds, I have frequently seen the furniture split, and articles which were veneered considerably damaged; the veneering in some cases being curled up like dried sheets of paper. Books left closed on the table at night would be found on the following morning completely opened, and each leaf standing up as if it had been highly stiffened with gum. At such times glass tumblers would break, apparently of their own accord; and I have known one slight tap given to a tumbler made of blown-glass, not only to break it, but, as if by sympathy, others remotely placed in different parts of the room.

When in the latitude of the Cape de Verde Islands on former occasions, at about this season of the year, and with the same hazy appearance, I have succeeded in obtaining some of the red Atlantic dust which is found to fall upon the rigging and decks of vessels. This dust was supposed for a long time to be carried by the north-east trade wind from the desert of Africa into the Atlantic; but it has been shown more recently, by Professor Ehrenberg, to consist, in great part, of infusoria with siliceous shields, and of the siliceous tissue of plants. Although many species of infusoria peculiar to Africa are known to Professor Ehrenberg, he has, I believe, found none of those in this Red Atlantic Dust examined by him. But, on the other hand, he has discovered in it two species hitherto known to him as living only in South America. At the season when this dust is so very plentiful in the air about the Cape de Verde Islands, the valley of the Orinoco is dry; and as the strong winds which sweep at that period of the year, over the valley of the Orinoco, are known to blow towards the Southern Andes, at the time when much vapour is condensed on that chain, and strong ascending currents of air are thereby created, it is held by writers on the Trade Winds, that this dust is carried to the eastward by an upper current of air, which again naturally falls to the earth, where the lower, or north-eastern, current commences.

In accordance with the above theory, Lieutenant Maury, of the United States Navy, concludes, with much apparent confidence, that this Red Atlantic Dust comes originally from South America; and it is even stated that it is carried by the south-west or upper current over Africa, and that some of this dust has even reached Germany and other parts of Europe.

It certainly is one of the most interesting phenomena of nature, throwing great light on the aërial currents, and one of which there are too many attesting witnesses to cause it to be doubted.

This Red Atlantic Dust has often fallen on ship's decks, when even one thousand miles distant from the African coast, and at points upwards of 1500 miles distant from each other in a north and south direction; showing over what an immense area of the Atlantic this phenomenon may be observed.

I can easily believe that vessels have run on shore, owing to the obscurity of the atmosphere, in this part of the ocean, for I have observed that large vessels were hardly visible at the distance of a mile from this cause; and navigators must have suffered great anxiety from the difficulty of making good observations at this, our winter season, in those latitudes.

After an experience of seven years on the West Coast of Africa, I have no hesitation in stating that the feeling of a Harmattan wind is very different from that of the north-east trade in the region just referred to.

On approaching the Equator, we were informed that some more of the drinking water was damaged, that the passengers were, in consequence, placed upon an allowance of one pint of water each per diem, and that we were to take charge of this allowance ourselves. The water was placed at the cabin-doors at six o'clock in the morning; and from the time we were put on short allowance of water, there was very little sleep on board of the ship after four o'clock in the morning; for every one was on the look-out, and, if one did not open the door of one's cabin and seize the water the moment it was placed there, it disappeared immediately;—there was no redress, and no more water to be had until the next morning.

Under these circumstances the children, of course, asked for more water than before; and young Frank Indigo recommended his companions to eat ham, bacon, in fact anything salt, "because then, you know, they must give you water."

The weather was getting warmer every hour, while we had the gratification of knowing that the liquids were decreasing rapidly; after the tenth day at sea, there was not a bottle of soda-water on board the "Ireland," bound to Calcutta, in the hot season.

On crossing the Equator, there were great

inquiries for old Father Neptune, but the captain thought it was judicious to bribe him not to visit the "Ireland," as the ceremony of shaving so many young ladies would have created quite a scene. So we found ourselves in another hemisphere without the occurrence of anything more amusing than the old trick of an aged tar exhibiting the "line" through a battered telescope; and the day was pretty well spent before the younger passengers discovered that the old wag had been inducing them to look at a thread of a spider's web instead of the Equator. The first visit to the Ocean reveals such mysteries that the human mind is prepared to entertain great absurdities as sublime truths.

From the time of passing the Cape de Verde Islands, the younger ladies had taken considerable interest in the Southern Cross. It was really a beautiful sight, as we proceeded rapidly to the south, under the power of steam, to see some of these fair maidens, night after night, sitting on the deck, gazing in silent admiration on the glorious firmament, spangled with the starry hosts.

Some of these fair girls had not been out of

England before; and one, I remember well, had never seen the Ocean until she beheld it in its fury from the deck of the "Ireland," when we made our first start from England. Those who have visited the Southern Hemisphere, and seen the emblem of Christianity standing alone in the heavens, pointing to the South Pole, may imagine the effect of this glorious panorama on the minds of these young girls.

The eye looks in vain for another constellation to rest upon; it is to the glorious revolving Cross that the Southern Hemisphere is indebted for its celestial beauty; and I have never been able to look upon it without thinking what must have been the feelings of Bartholomew Diaz, of Vasco de Gama, and their followers, who, as they bent their way to the dark pole, perceived this emblem of their faith dominant in the South:—

> "Ja descoberto tinhamos diante
> La no novo hemispherio nova estrella,
> Não vista de outra gente."

> "In this new hemisphere we first perceived
> A constellation great and brilliant,
> By all, but Lusians, hitherto unseen."

J. Musgrave's translation of the *Lusiad.*

The ladies never appeared tired of asking questions relative to the heavens; every book treating on astronomy, which could be discovered on board the vessel, was eagerly examined; and those gentlemen who were privileged to be present at the "star meetings" found both instruction and rational amusement, while some who had only studied the heavens before in a cursory manner, or even with scientific objects, were really surprised at the practical knowledge acquired by the young ladies in a few evenings.

One of these young ladies, and she was by no means a "blue stocking," informed us that her brother, who was a naval officer, had explained to her how both the Great Bear, in the north, and the Southern Cross, in the south, might be used for correcting the variation of the compass. When called upon one evening, with the compass before her, she very clearly pointed out how, with the Pole Star in the northern hemisphere, the variation of the needle may be ascertained within tolerable limits.

A few evenings afterwards, on coming on deck, after tea, the Southern Cross was observed standing nearly upright, but inverted; that is to say, approaching its lower culmination. The same young lady held a plumb line, made of a bullet and silken thread, before her eye, until the two extreme stars of the Cross came to the meridian, nearly pointing out the true south, by which our fair navigator read off the variation of the needle very correctly.

After this, I happened to state that both the Great Bear and the Southern Cross were clocks in the heavens for the use of those inhabiting the torrid zone, and each of them served the same purpose for the inhabitants of their own hemispheres. I was immediately called upon to explain my statement, and induced to give the following account of the manner of telling the hour by the Southern Cross :—

There can be little difficulty in remembering that, at the southern winter solstice, on the 21st of June, the right ascension of the sun is *six hours;* at the northern autumnal equinox, on the 21st of September, *twelve hours;* at the southern summer solstice, on the 21st of December, *eighteen hours;* and at the northern vernal equinox, on the 21st of March, *twenty-four hours*, very nearly : consequently we may say that the daily increase of the right ascension of the sun, the whole year round, is, on an average, *almost four minutes.*

If, therefore, I wish to know the sun's right ascension on the 1st of July, I recollect that at the last solstice, on the 21st of June, it was *six hours.* From this date to the 1st of July, ten days will have elapsed, which, multiplied by the daily increase, four minutes, makes its accumulation forty minutes, which, added to the six hours of right ascension attained by the sun on the 21st of June, gives a right ascension of six hours, forty minutes, on the day proposed.

Having obtained the right ascension of the sun, I have only to subtract that from the mean right ascension of the two antarctic pointers, *a* and γ Crucis, which being twelve hours, nineteen minutes, may easily be remembered.

"Do I make myself understood, ladies?"

"Oh, yes!"

"On the present occasion we have to subtract six hours, forty minutes, from twelve hours, nineteen minutes: which will leave five hours, thirty-nine minutes."

"Exactly so!"

"And that five hours, thirty-nine minutes, is P.M. time, when the Southern Cross will be upright on the meridian, on the day proposed, viz., the 1st of July."

"Well! this is Christmas Eve; what time was the Southern Cross on the meridian?"

"At the southern solstice, on the 21st of December, the right ascension of the sun was *eighteen hours;* from that date to the present, three days have elapsed."

"Yes—quite right."

"That will make the right ascension of the sun to-day, eighteen hours, twelve minutes; but how can we subtract that from twelve hours, nineteen minutes?"

"A very correct question; you must increase the right ascension of the pointers, in this and similar cases, by twenty-four hours, making it thirty-six hours, nineteen minutes, from which subtracting the right ascension for to-day, will give eighteen hours, twelve minutes, the time of the upper culmination of the Cross, counting from yesterday at noon, as you added twenty-four hours to the right ascension of the pointers; consequently the Cross was upright at twelve minutes past six o'clock this morning, and nearly twelve hours afterwards, it was at its lower culmination, when you saw our fair navigator correct the variation of the compass by it."

In this way the Southern Cross became an objcct of great admiration to the ladies, and they were soon able to estimate the time from it in any position.

The passengers in general made themselves agreeable to each other, and therefore many of our discomforts were made light of. This was not the case in other vessels belonging to the W.S.L. Line, and hence the disagreeable scenes which took place on board of them.

The ladies formed themselves into singing classes, under the direction of one of the reverend gentlemen passengers. Some of the gentlemen gave us their experience as travellers. One medical man gave us a lecture on the eye, and other subjects. Another young friend favoured us with an account of his ascent of the Nile, as far as Kartun. In this manner the day was got through, while in the evening, when tired of dancing, we gathered round the Captain on the poop, and there spent a pleasant hour or two in listening to some tale from him, or a song from the ladies.

The "Bill of Fare," in consequence of the destruction of our poultry from sheer neglect, became beautifully less; and, indeed, after the first fortnight, no dish left the table with anything on it—a pretty clear proof that the table was not well supplied. About the same time puddings were discontinued, in consequence of the head steward having thrown a dish containing an uncooked pudding at the baker's head. This placed the baker on the doctor's list, and stopped fresh bread for the cabin. All these trials were very severe on the children, of whom there were an unusual number on board. Still we all had some delicacies for the voyage, and these were cheerfully divided among the little ones.

At last the drinking water got very bad, the pint allowed to us being really as thick as the coffee, and looking very much like a dose of rhubarb, from the immense quantity of iron rust which it contained. It became so bad that it was impossible to drink without filtering it through blotting paper, an interesting occupation, which engaged the gentlemen's attention for some hours per diem. Here was another instance of neglect, the water-tanks having been filled without being cleaned. The officers of the ship said that they had never heard of white-washing the tanks inside with lime, to keep the water pure, and that the rust was always left in the tanks to purify their contents. I thought, after this, that a man might learn something new every day.

Our usual amusements began to tire us, and the increasing discomforts made us all long for the Cape of Good Hope, for we were becoming very discontented with the vessel, and began to give our feelings expression; when one day, while at lunch, where every one looked as if a little change of scene would do him good, there was a sudden cry of "Fire!—the ship's on fire!"

"Oh, where?—where?"

For a moment there was a scene of confusion, easier to imagine than to describe—

"Then shrieked the timid, and stood still the brave."

The Captain was at his post immediately; and it was soon discovered that the head of the main-mast was on fire.

The ship was at the time under steam, and all the sails were furled, it being a dead calm. The funnel was too close to the main-mast; and, as the vessel steamed ahead, there not being a breath of air, of course the smoke and heat from the funnel struck the main-mast and set it on fire.

The energetic exertions and cool example of the commander were not lost upon his subordinates, who ably seconded him. The chief officer greatly distinguished himself; as, indeed, did all the officers. The spars and burning rigging falling on some hay placed on the main hatchway, caused a blaze and considerable smoke, which made us imagine at one time that the ship was on fire in the main hold; but fortunately this was not the case.

The steam being up, we soon had a good supply of water from the engine-room, by means of a small auxiliary engine, called a "donkey engine," I suppose from the fact of its making a braying noise like that much-abused animal.

Water was got aloft, and poured over the sails, many of the men, as well as the chief officer, working on the hot-iron crosstrees at the mast-head, in the thick stifling smoke from the funnel, at the risk of their lives.

For some short time there was considerable fear that the fire would master us; but by the strenuous exertions of all, and the meritorious efforts of the crew, the fiery element was subdued. The only damage suffered was the loss of two sails, which were entirely burned, and the head of the main mast seriously charred.

In the middle of the fire, one of the gentlemen passengers, who had become deranged, and was in consequence confined to his cabin, finding his keeper absent, and alarmed by the confusion in the Saloon, rushed into it, among the ladies, with only one garment on him, and a large carving-knife in his hand. I need not say that the Saloon was instantly cleared.

At this moment the position of the ladies was anything but pleasant: a fire raging on deck, from which they did not know how soon they would be called upon to escape by the boats of the ship, which could not have held half the persons on board; and in the Saloon a raging maniac brandishing a large knife, by which he kept the cabin clear against all comers, and at the same time confined the ladies to their state-rooms.

As soon as the fire was got under, attention was turned to the disarming and securing of the poor maniac, when the "general" proposed getting his sword, and cutting the poor creature down; but younger heads and kinder hearts overruled this.

Some of the gentlemen promised to assist the doctor; and, having taken their stations, gradually closed on the poor sufferer; while the surgeon, conversing with his patient, and keeping him under the influence of his calm eye, approached and disarmed him. He was then easily secured, and confined in his cabin, until so much improved that, on approaching the Cape, he was allowed to roam about the decks, molesting no one. How different might have been his fate had violence been used to him during the temporary absence of reason!

Thankful, indeed, were we that the fire did not take place at night; in the consequent confusion, what accidents might not have happened? But He in whose "hands our times are" suited our trial to our means.

I observed that all were more contented with the ship after this exciting scene; but, nevertheless, we were exceedingly glad when, ten days after escaping from this great danger, we arrived in Table Bay, and anchored off Cape Town, the capital of the colony, grateful to that Merciful Providence who had led us so far safely on our journey.

CHAPTER III.

W.S.L., Worst Steam Line—Table Mountain—The Tablecloth is Spread—Pic-nic to Constantia—Careless Smoking—Cape Wines—The "Ireland" Proceeds to India—Melancholy Forebodings—Midnight Alarm in Simon's Bay—The Cape Observatory.

At noon of the last day in the month of January, 1857, the "Ireland" cast anchor in Table Bay, which was crowded with vessels of all sizes and under every flag. Even the national ensign of England, with the three talismanic letters, W.S.L., in glaring yellow, was seen flying at the mizen-peak of a steamer, recognized as the "England," a sister ship to the "Ireland," and belonging to the same line, well known at the Cape of Good Hope as the "worst steam line" which has yet called at that great turning point in the navigation between the East and the West.

Immediately on our anchoring, some of the passengers of the "England" came on board, who informed us that they were on the way to Europe, and that, between Mauritius and the Cape, they had fallen in with the tail-end of a hurricane, which had placed them in considerable danger, but that, having repaired damages, they were going to start for England in a few hours' time. Many of our passengers seized the opportunity to convey to their friends the intelligence of their safe arrival as far as the Cape of Good Hope.

Of course there was a comparison of "notes" as to the state of these two vessels, and we found that we were not worse off than the passengers on board our sister ship. We afterwards learned, from persons residing at the Cape, who had come in the "England" on her outward voyage, that previous to their arrival at Cape Town, they ran entirely out of drinking water, and that, on their making the harbour, they had to telegraph to the signal staff to send them water, by which means a water-tank was sent to them before their arrival. They had a large number of soldiers on board on that occasion, and it was stated that the military officers had to take matters in their own hands as far as the discipline of the stewards was concerned.

Fortunately, these two vessels were commanded by gentlemanly, considerate officers, and their tact and temper kept the discontent within reasonable bounds. With another vessel, belonging to the same line, matters took a different course, and on her arrival at the Cape of Good Hope the passengers were obliged to bind the commander to keep the peace towards them for the remainder of the voyage. The commander of the "Ireland" used his best endeavours to make the passage from England in thirty-five days; but we were forty-three days on the voyage, and would have been longer had we not been favoured by slants of wind, which, under ordinary circumstances, we could not have expected on the route adopted. The real fact was that the vessels were not fitted with sufficiently powerful machinery, and the space which ought to have been devoted to fuel was appropriated for cargo.

On arriving at Table Bay, our attention was drawn to a beautiful phenomenon of nature, by which Cape Town is supplied with water, and of which the following is a brief description :—

Table Mountain, under which Cape Town is built, is the terminus of a ridge of high land which covers a considerable portion of the promontory of the Cape of Good Hope. The side of this mountain, facing the north-west, and immediately behind the town, is perpendicular, and about 4000 feet in height. From the basin of Table Bay, during that portion of the twenty-four hours in which the air is warmer than the water, there is a considerable evaporation, which saturates the warm air overhanging the basin. The air, saturated with this moisture, rising to the edge of the cliff or summit of Table Mountain, meets with a cold polar current of air in the form of the prevalent south-east wind, by which it is immediately condensed into a cloud, and then precipitated on the ridge in the shape of dew or rain, according to the relative difference of temperature of the two currents of air. Thence, falling down the face or perpendicular side of the mountain, this deposit of dew or rain forms a stream of cool sparkling water, which affords an abundant supply to the 30,000 inhabitants of Cape Town, and the numerous ships that make this their port of call. From the harbour this white cloud appears as if ever pouring over the edge of the ridge, and never able to attain its object, the foot of the mountain. When dense, so as to entirely cover the top of Table Mountain, it is the precursor of a storm; so that, when bad weather is expected, it is usual to say that "the table-cloth is spread."

While engaged in looking at this beautiful phenomenon of nature, the increasing size of the table-cloth on the mountain warned us of the coming storm, and hastened us in our efforts to reach the shore. As there were a number of ladies and children on board the vessel having no gentlemen to assist them, and all anxious to reach the shore, after a passage during which they had suffered considerable privations, my wife made an offer of my services to provide accommodation for them at Cape Town, and render them any little assistance during their short stay in harbour. Accordingly our party was soon formed; a large shore-boat was provided, and we found ourselves on shore at Cape Town, and assembled at the custom-house, where the ladies had to remain until accommodation was provided for them. In consequence of there being so many vessels in harbour, the hotels, which are remarkably good, were full. After some little difficulty, always to be encountered in a strange town where one does not know one street from another, we succeeded in discovering two houses in which our large party could be accommodated as boarders, and where we were rendered very comfortable during our stay. The following day was devoted to viewing the town, already so often described, when the younger ladies discovered that they had left England without "quite a number" of little trifles which afforded them an opportunity of parting with their pin-money, and at the same time drawing a comparison of the value of "trifles" in England and in her Colonies. In the evening we had a visit from the young gentlemen passengers, when we were asked to join a pic-nic, to see one of the wine-producing estates. Preliminaries were soon arranged, and on the next morning a private omnibus (if I may use such an expression), with four beautiful horses, made its appearance at the door of our boarding-house. The hour was early, five in the morning, and this was supposed to afford an excuse for sundry performances on a key bugle, which hastened our departure, and considerably disturbed the neighbourhood. Adding our contribution to the already large supplies of edibles on the omnibus, and with the ladies comfortably seated inside, and the gentlemen on the outside, away we started for Constantia, the well-known estate of the hospitable family of the Vanreenans.

The gale, which had been blowing since our arrival, was at an end; the rain which had fallen had laid the red dust on the roads, which is the subject of great annoyance to the residents. The morning was cool, the air bracing and exhilarating to the spirits. Nature appeared to have put on her most smiling aspect to welcome us to this portion of her domain. And, in short, it was one of those charming mornings, so prevalent at the Cape, when the better nature of man will rise with the song of the birds in gratitude to the Divine Maker of all.

So sudden and so great a change from the confinement and discomfort of a vessel had a corresponding effect on us all; and, as the fleet horses dashed along, we fully enjoyed the scenes of quiet beauty, and the picturesque views which the road to Constantia revealed to us in that sunny morning.

There was not a disagreeable person in the party; all the agreeables had been gathered together, and the contrary natures had been excluded. The jest and quick repartee followed each other in rapid succession; all were smiles, and sorrow and sadness appeared to have lost their existence for that day.

Strange that we had been so long together, and had not until that morning learned the better part of each other's nature. How many surprises there were that day! Some learned that they were related by family ties, others that they were close neighbours in "the Old Country," and all that from that day forth they felt interested in each other's career.

Arrived at Constantia, we found the whole of those persons engaged on the estate in great commotion, for here, in this lovely spot, the frightful element "Fire," from which we had so lately escaped, had been doing considerable destruction; and, although the fire had been overcome, it was not known how soon it might break out again.

It appeared that the fire originated from one of the natives employed on the estate having carelessly thrown away the ashes of his pipe; these smouldered for a time, and the vegetation at that season being dry, when once inflamed, soon created an alarming conflagration, which rapidly assumed gigantic proportions, threatening to destroy all the surrounding estates. Fortunately the heavy rain of the previous night had somewhat arrested the progress of the fire, but, as the sun rose and the vegetation dried, it required constant vigilance to prevent the fire breaking out again.

In this state of things, of course our happy party could not think of intruding on these good people in their distress. But being politely offered the use of the grounds, we outspanned our horses, procured water, milk, and eggs, and, having some good housewives among the party, we enjoyed a most comfortable breakfast of our own providing.

The day was spent in rambling over the country, and making ourselves somewhat acquainted with the wine-growing of the colony. We were informed that the vine, from the grapes of which the delicious Constantia wine is produced, will only grow upon this estate, from which it derives its name, and only on certain portions of it where the soil is said to be of a quality peculiar to a few localities of this district.

The grape with which the wine is coloured is grown in a part of the estate set aside for that purpose, and appeared to us dryer and more stony than other localities.

The Cape, or South African, wines have been received with considerable favour in the English market, and are recommended in all our hospitals for their purity and absence of spirit.

The export of wine from the Cape has increased from 106,067 gallons, in 1854, to 797,092 gallons, in 1857; and during that period, in consequence of the failure of the grape in Europe, the price of the wine has increased three-fold;—a cask of Cape wine, which could be purchased formerly in England for eighteen pounds, now fetching fifty-four pounds sterling.

At the present moment, I am inclined to think that the merchants give too high a price to the producers to enable us to benefit to the extent that we should in England from the large supplies of wine which we may obtain from the Cape. But now that roads through newly-discovered mountain passes are opening up new districts suitable for the production of wine, such as the Oudts horn, and many others, the increased supply will naturally decrease its cost in the market.

There is an earthy taste in the South African wines, which greatly reduces their value; as this is not inherent to the grape, but simply the effect of the red dust of the district with which the grapes are covered, more attention in the manufacture of the wines will obviate this objection, and place them in that position in the markets of Europe to which their intrinsic merit entitle them.

After passing a most agreeable day, we returned

to Cape Town, as the shades of evening were closing in, and night was about to spread her mantle over the forest of masts floating in Table Bay.

In two days afterwards the "Ireland" was away on her course to India, bearing with her those who were to take part in the great Indian drama. The merry-hearted whip, who handled the ribbons so gracefully; the mother, with her loving children; the maidens, with their mirthful laughter; the soldier, with his gallant bearing; the beardless boys, panting for glory and this world's renown, who joined us on that festive day at Constantia—where are they?

Foremost amongst the stormers of Lucknow the soldiers fell; the merry-hearted whip died, homeward bound, from the effects of his fearful wounds; the mother, after watching over her babes through dangers worse than death, arrived in safety at Calcutta, then drooped and died. The maidens—one, the loveliest of them all, was seized with cholera on her arrival in India; her beauty vanished and her spirit fled—some are wedded, while others perished—ask not how.

On landing at Cape Town, I had made inquiries

for the Naval Commander-in-chief, and was informed that Commodore Trotter was up the Mozambique Channel. In the absence of the chief, I applied to the officer in charge of the naval station, when I found that, although orders had been sent out to the Cape, at the request of the Foreign Office, to forward me to my Post in one of Her Majesty's ships, no definite steps had been taken for that purpose.

When the Admiralty orders for the conveyance of Her Majesty's Consul for Mozambique to his Post, in a ship of war, reached Simon's Town, it appears there was, at that time, the miserable remains of a vessel lying in the harbour, which, in former times, did duty as a tender to the ship of the senior officer, but, owing to her being unseaworthy, she had been condemned. As the orders were imperative, it was supposed that an officer of some standing, commanding a large steamer, would have to convey me to Mozambique; as the steamer in question, from her great expenditure of coals, was worse than useless on the Cape station, to which all the coals used have to be carried from England at a great expense. This steamer was a remarkably good sailor, and might have been usefully employed under canvas, in the Mozambique Channel, instead of lying, month after month, at Simon's Bay doing nothing.

The Mozambique Channel is looked upon as one of the most unhealthy stations in the world; and, therefore, it is but natural that a naval officer, who has arrived at a position on the Navy List, where he knows that seniority will alone advance him, should hesitate to go to a part of the world where he is likely to make a vacancy. On the return of the Commodore, the destination of the large steamer was pretty well indicated, and, therefore, it was suggested that the old condemned schooner "Dart" should be fitted out to take the Consul to Mozambique, and, by her imposing appearance in that port, awe the slave-dealers of Eastern Africa.

Accordingly, a lieutenant and a party of men were ordered on board the "Dart;" her old sails were bent, and with the assistance of some coils of rope, a few buckets of tar, two or three pounds of putty, and the expenditure of a pot or two of black paint, all supplied by order from Her Majesty's Dockyard at Simon's Town, the "Dart" began to look quite smart. The loftier spars were put in their places, the lighter yards thrown across, the masts nicely stayed, the yards squared, ropes hauled taut—long, low, and rakish; with a blue ensign abaft, and a long blue pennant at the mast head, she looked "quite the thing."

Many smiled at the "Consul's Yacht" (as I was told they called the "old Dart done up"); some shook their heads, and ventured to doubt if the Consul would ever reach his Post in her, and all were on the look out for the arrival of the "Ireland," when suddenly, one night, there was heard, over the harbour of Simon's Town, a cry of distress proceeding from the "old Dart done up." "Help! help! for heaven's sake, the Consul's Yacht is sinking." Immediately, the boatswain's mate's whistles were heard on board of all the men-of-war in the harbour. "Away there, boat's crews—away, there, away!" "Hurry up, lads; that d—d thing of paint and putty is going down at her anchors!!"

By the exertions of those on board, pumping and baling with buckets, the "old Dart" was kept afloat until the men-of-war's boat towed her into shallow water, when she was again dismantled, being pronounced not even fit for a "Consul's Yacht."

This, I found, was the only step that had been taken towards forwarding me to my Post, where the slave-trade, in its most revolting form, was carried on without a hope of being checked, but by my intervention as the British Consul.

As a large amount of *specie* was expected from England, which would have to be carried by one of Her Majesty's ships from Simon's Bay to Algoa Bay, the large steamer was compelled to remain for this important service, and Her Majesty's Consul for Mozambique was detained at the Cape of Good Hope for more than five months, the greater portion of which time three steam-ships of war were lying in Simon's, or Table, or Algoa Bay. To those who may not be initiated in the subject of the carriage of *specie*, I ought to explain that the Captains of Her Majesty's ships receive a certain per centage on all *specie* carried by the vessel which they command; while, for carrying Consuls, and other public servants, they receive only a fairly remunerative amount of table-money to compensate them for any expense they may have been put to in entertaining their guest.

When head money for pirates was found to be a premium for murder, it was very properly abolished. Similarly, let us hope that freight-money for the carriage of gold and silver will no longer be an inducement to the neglect of the public service.

As the movements of the squadron at the Cape were wrapt in the most sublime mystery, it was quite impossible to anticipate the distant period when one of Her Majesty's ships could be placed at my disposal.

Under these circumstances, finding that my future movements were *in nubibus*, I resolved to take time by the forelock. Having made the acquaintance of Mr. Thomas Maclear, F.R.S., the Astronomer Royal for the Cape of Good Hope, and, through the courtesy of the Honourable Mr. Field, Collector of the Customs, being allowed to take my scientific instruments out of the Custom House, I had my magnetic instruments conveyed to the Royal Observatory, where Mr. Maclear, with that generous aid which he is always ready to afford in the cause of science, had a room placed at my disposal. Lodgings were procured near the Observatory, and many agreeable hours were passed by my wife and myself in the society of Mr. and Mrs. Maclear, and their amiable and highly intelligent family, whose unvarying kindness and attention to us, while resident at the Cape, will never be forgotten.

CHAPTER IV.

Table Bay—Breakwater to be Built—Harbour of Refuge—Policy of Sir George Grey—Proposal for Carrying the Mail to the Cape by way of Aden—Discovery of Coal on the Zambesi—Its Effects on the Future of South and East Africa—Absence of Trees at Cape Town—Climate of the Cape.

SINCE the Portuguese voyagers, Bartholomew Diaz and Vasco de Gama, rounded the Cape of Good Hope, and opened to the commerce of Europe, by way of the Southern Ocean, the rich and still undeveloped countries of the East, what magnificent ships of war, and fleets of merchantmen—chartered with the good, the fair, and the brave—have sailed past that Cape of Tempests, finding, in the midst of that stormy sea, no haven of rest from the gale, no harbour of refuge from the hurricane!

During the four hundred years which have passed since the gorgeous panorama of the East was made known to Europe by the immortal actors in the Portuguese Era of Conquest, what numbers of human beings have perished, what untold riches have been engulphed around that stormy headland!

On the great ocean route from Europe to India, if we except Port Louis, in the Island of Mauritius, there is not one harbour containing dry docks, and the necessary accommodation for repairing in security the hulls of the immense merchant fleets, of sailing and steam-ships, which are for ever ploughing the watery waste which lies between the East and the West. That such a great necessity should so long have existed, at such an important turning point of navigation as that of the Cape of Good Hope, can only be accounted for by the great natural difficulties to be overcome in the formation of a harbour of refuge having the necessary capabilities to supply the wants of the large amount of shipping passing the Cape.

Lying in a great line of commerce and navigation, and, from the recent rapid development of internal communication by the construction of roads, which will be immediately followed by railroads, already commenced, it requires only a judicious expenditure of money, rendering Table Bay a safe, accessible, and quiet harbour, to make Cape Town a port of great wealth, an emporium for the East and the West, and the outlet for the rich and varied productions of Southern Africa. From time to time projects have been set on foot for this purpose, but it has been reserved for the era of Colonial Self-Government to introduce a plan, magnificent in conception, practicable in details, and incalculable in results, for the purpose of rendering Table Bay a safe harbour at all times and seasons.

The principal wants which will be supplied by this great undertaking are:—

1st. A harbour easy of access, and safe at all times and seasons for the commerce between the East and the West.

2nd. A refuge for vessels repairing and refitting; and—

3rd. A naval station for the purpose of protecting the navigation to India, China, and Australia in time of war.

Table Bay, with its roadstead, is a bight facing the north, and protected on the west by the promontory of the Lion's Rump, running due north about one mile and a half. On the south-east it is a flat shore. Cape Town lies in the south-west or most sheltered part of the bay; and if an imaginary line be drawn from Mouille Point due east, until it cuts the opposite shore, it will give to this anchorage an extent of three miles. Nature has already provided for it an admirable shelter, by the promontory on the west, from which point of the compass to north it is exposed to the most violent local winds, which prevail chiefly in the months of June, July, and August, occasionally occurring with fatal violence in other months of the year. These winds are accompanied by a very heavy swell, which, driven into a narrow bay, with no outlet, forms a sea dangerous to shipping, during the continuance of which vessels are unable to discharge or receive cargoes. Owing to there being no sheltered quays, the loading and discharging of ships is performed by means of lighters. The aggregate expense arising from loss of vessels, detention of shipping, conveyance of goods and passengers by lighters and boats, may be fairly stated at 30,000*l.* sterling per annum, nearly equivalent to 900,000*l.* of capital; which, with the value of the land which will be reclaimed by the proposed works, and the rental of the sea frontage of quays and wharves, will more than cover the expense of outlay.

The funds for the necessary outlay have already been provided by the Colonial Parliament, by "An Act for Constructing a Breakwater, to form a Harbour of Refuge in Table Bay, and otherwise improving the said harbour."

A comprehensive plan for the construction of the harbour was some time since prepared by Captain James Vetch, R.E., F.R.S., Engineer to the Admiralty in England.

Mr. Coode, Engineer to the Portland breakwater, has been appointed Engineer-in-chief, resident in England.

Mr. Arthur Thomas Andrews, Civil Engineer, of considerable practice, and possessing the confidence of Mr. Coode, has been appointed Resident

Engineer, and left England, accompanied by an agent of the contractor for the works, for Cape Town, in March of this year (1859).

The facilities for the construction of the Breakwaters are great; stone of admirable quality may be conveyed from the quarries on a tramway to the works, and there are about 600 local convicts who may be profitably employed on this great undertaking

From the Engineer-in-chief being engaged in the construction of Portland breakwater, it may be fairly anticipated that the practical experience obtained there will be beneficially applied to an undertaking redounding to the energy of the Cape Colony, beneficial to the commerce of all nations, and a lasting monument of the protective power of Imperial Britain.

Similar works are contemplated at Port Elizabeth, in Algoa Bay; and a railway has been commenced in Cape Town, which will eventually form a grand trunk line in South Eastern Africa. Numerous minor works, such as bridges, convict-stations, and other public buildings, are in the course of execution, while mountain passes are being explored for the purpose of carrying roads through them, which will give access to districts which, for the want of means of transit, have hitherto been shut up. These undertakings will not only provide employment for great numbers of the working-classes for many years to come, but will effectually develop the agricultural and commercial resources of the colony.

The dangers which formerly existed to the colonists, from the frequent Kaffir eruptions, may be fairly stated as now ended; for the enlightened policy adopted by the Imperial Government, suggested and firmly carried out by the present governor, Sir George Grey, has entirely broken up the former formidable power of the Kaffir chiefs, and has made them, in the hands of the governor, willing instruments for the gradual civilization of their people. The independence of the tribes no longer exists; one-third of them, forced by famine, brought on by their own imprudence, have migrated to the Cape Colony, where they seek for work, and imperfectly supply the wants of the colonists.

The present time, in view of the great and

varied public works undertaken in the colony, appears a most favourable period for emigration to the Cape of Good Hope; and as the Cape Colony has appropriated 50,000*l.* a year for the introduction of well-selected emigrants into the colony, and the governor has sent to England a gentleman of high official standing, and well acquainted with the requirements of the colony, as Emigration Commissioner, measures will be adopted for carrying out this object with a view to the true interests of the colony, by supplying it with an amount of labour commensurate with its wants.

Sir George Grey, in inviting the co-operation of the landed proprietors of the colony for the introduction of emigrants, writes on the 7th January, 1858:—"The present time is very favourable for making an effort in this direction. The rapid progress which the colony has recently made—the prospect of future immunity from the constantly recurring alarm of Kaffir outbreaks—the extraordinary development of the productive powers of the colony, notwithstanding the paucity of its population—the demonstration of its fitness for yielding the principal sources of agricultural wealth, grain, wine, and wool—and of its capabilities of consuming the productions of other countries in large and increasing quantities, as indicated by the returns of importations, and by the rank which it now holds in this respect among the colonies of Great Britain—all hold out great inducements to persons contemplating emigration from Great Britain to turn their attention to this country, and the strongest incentives to the government and people of the colony to avail themselves of such an opportunity of offering every encouragement to the best classes of emigrants to select it for their future home."

During my stay at Cape Town, I proposed that the mail should be carried from England to this colony by way of Aden, ensuring, in the first place, a greater certainty in the arrival of the mail, and the return of post in a shorter period; besides affording to the colony direct communication with the Portuguese Colonial Possessions and the Dominions of the Imâm of Muskat in Eastern Africa, by which an inter-colonial trade, highly renumerative to all parties, and truly beneficial to the Cape Colony, would be established.

But I regret to say that my plan was objected to, on the very narrow-minded ground that the neighbouring enterprising British Colony of Natal would be more directly benefited than the Cape people; and, more especially, that the Natal merchants would by that route receive their advices from England before the Cape merchants, and would also have the great advantages of the last quotations, both from the Cape and Natal markets, in addressing their correspondents, in England, which objections appeared to outweigh the advantages to be derived from a terminus to the route, and the opening out of the rich produce of Eastern Africa.

The experience of the last two years has proved what I then predicted, viz., that the steam communication between the Cape Colony and Natal would pay; for now, instead of there being only one steamer, there are no less than three on that line. The communication by steamer being thus successfully established between the Cape of Good Hope and Port Natal, it remains only to complete it by establishing a line from Natal to Aden. The Natal people have the matter now entirely in their own hands; and I have so great confidence in their energy, that I feel assured that steamers will be running, before two years are over, between Natal and Aden, calling at Iniack Island (in Delagoa Bay), the mouths of the Zambesi, Mozambique, Zanzibar, and one of the outlets for the commerce of North Eastern Africa; throwing a brilliant ray of light to illumine the darkness of East Ethiopia; an advancement in civilization which the world will owe to the energy of the young and enterprising British Colony of Natal.

The recent discoveries of coal on the Zambesi have given an immediate practicability to the early development of the resources of South and Eastern Africa, which could scarcely have been anticipated a few years since.

It may not be generally known that Great Britain exports 700,000 tons of coal annually to the East of the Cape of Good Hope; and now that railroads are being introduced into the colonies of the Cape and Natal, and new steam lines of ships are coming into existence for the requirements of those young and thriving colonies, eager to place themselves in communication with neighbouring settlements, it is not too much to say that double the amount of fuel already named will be required to carry out these necessary projects, cramping them in their infancy by the enormous expense entailed in carrying fuel from England to those colonies.

In the colony of Natal it is true that a seam of coal has been discovered, which may be found, on more careful examination, to be of a quality and in quantity suitable for the already great demands for fuel of that colony, from its sugar, indigo, and other mills; and that in the same locality further discoveries of coal may be made; but until these points are satisfactorily cleared up, it is to us a subject of great interest, as well as thankfulness, that rich supplies of coal have been discovered by Dr. Livingstone on the Zambesi, with which that practical discoverer is now working the engine of his small steam launch, the "Ma Robert."

When it is stated that one British steam company, namely, the Peninsular and Oriental Steam Navigation Company, expend the enormous sum of 600,000*l.* per annum on coal alone, for the supply principally of their depôts at Aden, and other places to the east of the Cape of Good Hope, it ought to stimulate our colonists in South Africa to make diligent search for this valuable commodity.

Those now residing at Cape Town are aware of the serious item which fuel makes in the expenditure of a family; and, as the colonists increase, of course this must be looked forward to with serious consideration.

The first distinguishing feature in the country on landing at Cape Town, and even subsequently, after becoming more familiar with the locality, is the almost entire absence of trees. It is true that this want is in a fair way of being supplied by the active measures which have been adopted by all parties in surrounding their residences with the beautiful blue gum tree, which in ten years attains the height of from sixty to seventy feet, with a diameter of twelve inches. This tree affords an agreeable shade, and may be usefully employed, as the wood is hard, close grained, and resinous. But many years must elapse ere this laudable object, of giving a wooded appearance to Cape Town, is carried out.

The history of the Cape of Good Hope is already too well known to be even briefly alluded to here, and may be derived at any time from means which are open to all; but, without wishing to weary the reader, it will be necessary to give some account of the climate, and the present state of the revenue, imports, and exports of the colony.

In a letter addressed to the Honourable William Field, now Emigration Commissioner for the Cape Colony in England, Mr. Maclear, the Astronomer Royal at the Cape, writes, under date of September 9th, 1857:—

"In respect to the important subject of health, the leading feature of the Cape climate is remarkable. Perhaps there is no country on the face of the globe so free from those diseases which spring from putrid exhalations. Cholera, typhus, bilious, remitting, and yellow fevers are unknown. The explanation is found in the frequent refreshing winds which carry off deleterious matter, and diminish the depressing effects of summer heat. For this indulgence the Cape is indebted to its geographical position. Freely exposed to the breeze from the Southern and Atlantic oceans, it reaps the advantages which are sought in England by a residence on the coast.

"Contagious complaints, you are well aware, are far between; and when they do appear, they have been imported, and soon wear out from the same cause which checks malaria.

"Upon the whole, the Cape climate approaches closely to the climate of Madeira; indeed, the only difference seems to consist in the winds being stronger and more regular at the Cape."

The following table, compiled from observations made for 14 years under the immediate superintendence of Mr. Maclear, the Astronomer Royal, at the Royal Observatory, three miles from Cape Town, will give an accurate idea as regards the general character of the climate:—

Royal Observatory, Cape of Good Hope.

MEAN OF METEOROLOGICAL OBSERVATIONS, FROM 1842 TO 1856.

MONTHS.	Mean of each Month.	Highest and lowest of Maximum each Month.		Highest and lowest of Minimum each Month.	
January . . .	68·77	94·7	81·4	60·4	52·4
February . . .	68·99	97·4	78·6	61·6	51·5
March	66·29	91·2	77·8	55·6	46·7
April.	62·95	91·4	73·0	52·6	45·0
May	58·01	85·2	64·4	48·6	41·0
June.	55·35	77·2	65·5	44·6	37·7
July	54·57	75·4	62·7	44·2	38·0
August	51·21	76·8	62·2	45·1	38·0
September . . .	57·43	83·0	69·4	48·9	40·0
October. . . .	61·06	86·2	73·0	50·8	43·7
November . . .	64·28	93·6	72·6	56·8	46·0
December . . .	67·61	96·8	74·9	59·0	48·6
Mean . . .	61·71				

The mean temperature of England is 62°; and while the average temperature of the Cape of Good Hope is shown to be even below that of our own country, these colonists have not the extremes of temperature which we suffer in England, as the average temperature of their winter is but 14°.42 below that of summer.

From the foregoing observations it will be seen that not only as regards temperature itself, but also as to its diurnal and yearly range, and the amount of rain and wind, there is nothing in the climate unfavourable to the European constitution, but on the contrary. These observations, most carefully conducted, prove it to be a climate free from violent changes of heat and cold; and experience has proved that in many cases the change to the Cape climate has checked, if not entirely eradicated the early symptoms of *phthisis* in European, and more especially English subjects.

The climate is also peculiarly favourable for Emigrants; for, from its equable temperature, during ten months of the year, fire is only required for cooking purposes; and it will be at once apparent that this alone removes many of the hardships and expences attending emigration, to less genial climates.

While on the subject of emigration, it may be remarked that too much care cannot be used in the selection of emigrants for this colony. Provisions continue to be enormously high, showing that a more extensive cultivation of the soil is required, and at once pointing out the description of labour which ought to be introduced. House-rent is extravagantly high; and all classes have to struggle against the general dearness of the necessaries of life.

If the large supplies of native labour, introduced by Sir George Grey, can be turned to the cultivation of the soil, one of the great ends of all good government, the supply of cheap food for the people, will be the result.

Since 1852, the principle of self-government has been wisely accorded by the imperial government to the Colony of the Cape of Good Hope; and it appears really wonderful what an improvement has taken place in the development of the resources of the colony since that date, and the consequent increase of its revenue.

By a reference to the statistics of the colony, it will be seen that for six years previous to that important change in its government, the revenue was gradually decreasing. As soon as the affairs of the colony were left in the hands of the colonists, an impetus was given to the opening of new, and repairing of old, passes and roads, by which large tracts of country, scarcely accessible before, were brought into commercial relationship with the coast and shipping ports. The colonists knew the requirements of the colony; and the natural result was that a revenue which, in 1852, was 289,482*l.* sterling, became in the short space of five years, viz., 1857, 406,702*l.*—a striking proof of the benefit of colonial self-government.

To its temperate and genial climate the Cape Colony is indebted, in a great measure, for its prosperity; for it is this which enables it to produce such large quantities of wool and wine, and to breed sheep, cattle, and horses with such success.

The production of wool in this colony, in the year 1833, was 113,000lbs.; in twenty years it had increased to 7,700,000lbs. per annum; and since that date, in the short space of five years, it has more than doubled, being in 1858, 18,000,000lbs.; these are figures which require no comment.

The number of hides exported in 1853 was 5,278, and in 1856, 96,218; of sheep and goat skins, 168,708 were exported in 1854; and 766,000 of the same in 1856; showing at once the increase in cattle and sheep.

For many years American flour has been introduced, to supply the wants of the colonists; but lately this importation has almost entirely ceased, owing to greater attention having been paid to the cultivation of the soil, so that the colony has already commenced exporting to the neighbouring wealthy colony of Mauritius; having supplied that island in 1857, with 1,000,000 lbs. of flour, 800,000 lbs. of bran, 1,500 quarters of barley and beans, and 3,116 quarters of oats.

Without fatiguing the general reader with statistics, it may be briefly stated that, while the colony contains 126,930 square miles, or nearly 80,000,000 acres, there are at present only 186,292 acres under cultivation, showing at once its great power of increase.

CHAPTER V.

Further Detention at the Cape—Arrival of the "Frolic" from Mozambique—"John of the Coast"—New Naval Commander-in-Chief—Storm at the Cape—Courage of Cape Boatmen—Destruction of Shipping in Table Bay—Embark in the "Hermes"—Coast of Kaffraria—Well Watered and Beautiful Country.

I HAVE already stated that I had arrived at Cape Town on the last day in the month of January, since which date I had been using my best endeavours to induce the Naval authorities to send me on to Mozambique. But from some inexplicable cause I was detained at the Cape month after month.

At first the Commodore was absent. In about six weeks after my arrival he returned, and a month after that he had not made up his mind which of the steamers of his squadron to send up the Mozambique Channel. Then he intimated to me that it was the unhealthy season on the East Coast of Africa. To this I replied, that all seasons were alike to me, and that it was my duty to reach my Post immediately.

It was then stated that the governor, Sir George Grey, required the steamers. I waited on His Excellency, and found that one steamer was required for the service of the colony, to examine the St. John's River. I got into the mail cart, and proceeded to Simon's Town, a distance of twenty-two miles from Cape Town. At the end of my journey, I found that the Commodore wished to wait for the arrival of H.M.S. "Frolic," from the Mozambique Channel, and that my movements were as uncertain as ever.

The "Frolic" arrived, and in her a passenger from Mozambique, who was sent to officer's quarters at the naval hospital. I again repaired to Simon's Town, and found that the Illustrious Senhor from Mozambique had strongly recommended that no ship of war should be sent up the Mozambique Channel at that season, as it was so unhealthy. I was introduced by the Commodore to the Illustrious Senhor, who was recommended to me as a "very good fellow," a great friend of the English, and one who gave great information relative to the slave trade. The Commodore was pleased to say that the detention which had taken place would be all to my advantage, as I would be accompanied to Mozambique by the Illustrious Senhor, who had merely come to the Cape for the benefit of his health.

The Illustrious Senhor, whom I shall for the future call "John of the Coast," informed me that he had been ill for a long time, and that the Commodore had offered him a passage to the Cape when there, in H.M. frigate "Castor;" but that, having been apprized by his friends in London that I had left England, he determined to remain at Mozambique, and await my arrival at that place.

I thanked my newly made friend for his great consideration, and informed him that I had already learned his great kindness to my countrymen who called there in H.M. ships.

Subsequently, he told me that, having heard of

my arrival at the Cape, and being aware that no Cruiser would be sent up the Mozambique Channel until the return of the "Frolic," he had accepted the invitation of her Commander, and had come to the Cape to make my acquaintance, as he felt sure it would be mutually beneficial.

Acknowledging his great consideration, I asked him to pay me a visit as soon as he was sufficiently recovered to undertake the journey. In a fortnight's time he was my guest, and remained in that capacity during our further stay at the Cape.

"John of the Coast" informed me that he was the eldest son of a Portuguese officer, of very exalted rank, at Mozambique; that his father was a Brigadier in the Portuguese army, a man of great influence among the native chiefs in Eastern Africa, and that, like himself, he was very anxious that the Slave Trade should be abolished, and legitimate trade introduced.

My guest gave me great information relative to the country which I was about to visit, all of which, I afterwards found, was correct.

Time passed on, and the month of June

arrived, bringing the steamer "Charity" to Simon's Bay, with the Honourable Sir Frederick Grey, K.C.B., as Rear-admiral and Commander-in-chief of Her Majesty's naval forces on the East and West African stations. Her Majesty's steamer "Geyser" was immediately placed at my disposal, and ordered to Table Bay to embark myself and my baggage,

Whilst at anchor in Table Bay, the Commander of that vessel indulged in such extraordinary antics, that it was apparent to most people that he was suffering from an aberration of intellect, or from some other exciting cause, which rendered him totally incompetent to command the vessel in which the late Commodore had placed him as Acting Commander.

My baggage was on board the "Geyser," and everything was ready for our departure, when that vessel was ordered to Simon's Bay, under charge of the Senior Lieutenant, as it was found necessary to inquire into the extraordinary conduct of her Acting Commander; and the "Hermes" was ordered to receive my baggage and myself for conveyance to Mozambique.

On the eve of the departure of the "Geyser" from Table Bay for Simon's Bay, one of those terrific storms came on, which generally visit the Cape some time in the month of June. Fortunately, the "Geyser" had her steam up, and the officers succeeded in getting her out of Table Bay, after she had carried away both chain cables from the violence of the sea which sets into that anchorage with the commencement of a north-westerly gale.

When the chain cables of Her Majesty's ships (which are not insured) are carried away, it is certain that those supplied to merchantmen will not hold out, and therefore it will not be surprising to hear that the gale alluded to caused great destruction in Table Bay. When it commenced, there were thirty-three fine merchantmen, of different sizes, and under various flags, lying at anchor there, all more or less prepared for the bad weather which is expected at Table Bay in the winter months of the southern hemisphere.

For three days it blew with terrific violence, and during this time it was a sublime but melancholy spectacle to see the sport made of the works of man by the mighty power of the ocean which came tumbling into this bay.

But, on the other hand, it was a lofty and inspiring sight to witness the undaunted resolution with which the Cape boatmen laid out anchors to windward of the ships in distress, and then conveyed the strong coir elastic cables attached to them to hold on the parting vessels. During the height of the storm, in the fury of the hurricane, the great and good governor of the colony, Sir George Grey, was, by his presence and by his exertions, aiding these measures in the cause of humanity.

For the laying out of an anchor, and conveying a coir cable attached to it, the boatmen receive 150*l*. sterling, and well do they deserve that amount, for the risk is very great. During the storm, one vessel was charged 600*l*. for assistance of this sort, and it would be unwise to dispute the charges made by these people; for one moment's hesitation in supplying the required aid may result in the loss of a vessel. This is not the only danger, for when once a vessel gets adrift, there is no knowing what amount of damage she may do to other vessels, and the loss of how many of them she may cause.

Out of the thirty-three vessels lying in Table Bay at the commencement of the gale, eleven were blown on shore, most of which became total wrecks, and all of those that remained afloat were more or less severely damaged, besides costing a large amount for anchors and cables. Of course all this money is lost to the owners or underwriters. This one example will show the necessity for the Harbour of Refuge already referred to.

The gale was over, the "Hermes" reported ready for sea, and we impatient to start. After bidding farewell to our kind friends, the Maclears, the Chevalier Duprat and family, and Mr. and Mrs. George Frere, from all of whom we had received great kindness during our protracted stay at the Cape, we got into a carriage, and started off to Simon's Bay, where the "Hermes" was awaiting us. Our party consisted of Mrs. M'Leod, Mr. Soares, myself, and my wife's maid, Rosa Smith, of whom mention will frequently be made in the following pages.

A few miles before arriving at Simon's Town, just previous to descending to the sandy flats over which the public road passes, I desired the coachman to pull up for the purpose of showing my wife a sign over a wayside inn, which had struck my fancy amazingly.

As it was something novel in the way of advertising, I took a copy of it while the horses were breathing, and insert it for the benefit of the reader.

The house of refreshment rejoices in the name of "The Gentle Shepherd of Salisbury Plain," and the following inscription is placed on a large board, which swings about with a screeching noise, evidently with an eye to business :—

> "Multum in parvo! Pro bono publico!
> Entertainment for man and beast all of a row.
> Lekker kost as much as you please,
> Excellent beds without any fleas.
> Nos patriam fugimus: Now we are here,
> Vivimus, let us live by selling Beer.
> On dit, à boire et à manger ici,
> Come in and try it, whoever you be."

On arriving at Simon's Town, previous to embarking, I waited on the Admiral; and Sir

Frederick Grey being a man of business, a few minute's conversation with him placed me in possession of all the information relative to the Mozambique territory, in his office. While the "Hermes" was getting up her steam, the admiral's clerks were set to copy the documents which I selected as likely to be useful to me.

I had been endeavouring, without success, to learn something from the naval authorities relative to Mozambique, for more than five months, during which I was detained, most unwillingly on my part, at the Cape, and now a new chief arrived, who immediately placed a vessel at my disposal, and gave me the information I required. To me it is a subject of great satisfaction to meet with the right man in the right place.

Besides those already named as belonging to my party, an officer and thirty-three soldiers for Natal were passengers in the "Hermes;" and Mr. Daniel Cloete, a brother of the Recorder of Natal, who is well known for his lectures on that colony, was a guest of the ward-room officers of the ship.

Pacing the deck of the "Hermes," memory carried me back fourteen years, to the day when I first ascended her side in Port Royal Harbour, Jamaica, with my promotion into her as a midshipman, from the subordinate rank of a volunteer of the first class, now denominated a naval cadet. The old craft and I were no strangers; and I was glad to find that there was as nice a set of fellows in her as in former days. Captain Gordon set an example to all; and, indeed, I can never forget his great attention to our comfort while on board. My wife, from his hearty welcome, felt quite at home; and, although the old Symonite did roll uncommonly, we enjoyed the passage in her amazingly.

Captain Gordon was an old cruiser in these waters, having been Senior Lieutenant of a steamer during the Kaffir war; and, being well acquainted with the coast, he kept well in shore, and took great pleasure in pointing out to us every remarkable place on the passage to Natal.

One cannot help being struck with the park-like appearance of the land, when steaming along the coast of Kaffraria; a valuable territory, situated between our two colonies of the Cape and Natal, which, in the course of events, must become annexed to our South African possessions. Many parts of the country along this line of coast are truly picturesque, and all really beautiful. But until one arrives at the St. John's River, the country appears to be indifferently wooded, with the exception of a few places where magnificent timber-trees make their appearance. At the St. John's River, a visible change in the aspect of the country takes place. There the land, being a succession of terraces rising from the ocean, offers the most beautiful spots, already cleared away by the hand of nature, for the erection of residences, having for their back-grounds magnificent forests, while the sea view unfolds the boundless expanse of the Southern Ocean, through storm and calm, bearing on its bosom the argosies richly laden with the commerce of the East and the West.

From St. John's River to Port Natal there are one hundred and twenty-two rivers, all of which, of course, are not navigable; but many of them are more or less practicable for boats and small vessels, giving access, by water, to this rich country. Its value cannot be over-estimated, being exceedingly healthy, and having a climate in which the vegetable productions of the temperate and torrid zones may be raised side by side. The fact of there being one hundred and twenty-two rivers discharging themselves into the ocean, in a coast-line of one hundred and thirty miles, shows how beautifully the country is naturally irrigated. Man's energy is alone required to turn the virgin soil of this district into a land of plenty.

CHAPTER VI.

Arrive at Natal—The Bar—Proposed Harbour of Refuge—Wharves in the St. Lawrence—Railroad at Natal—D'Urban—Port Natal Harbour—Verulam—Pieter-Maritzburg—Slave Ship off Port Natal—The Havannah Slavers—Chamber of Commerce—Natal Waggon—"Daft Jemmy."

After a remarkably fine passage of five days from Simon's Town, the "Hermes" anchored off Port Natal on Wednesday, the 1st July, 1857.

In consequence of its having blown fresh from the northward and the eastward, the Bar was impassable, and we had no communication with the shore on that day, excepting by telegraph from the ship to the signal station on the Bluff, by means of which we informed the Natalians that there was an officer and thirty-three soldiers on board, and requested the authorities to send off boats to land this small party as soon as the Bar was practicable.

On Thursday the port boat, built as a life-boat, came alongside, but the Coxswain of her declined taking any passengers in consequence of the unsettled state of the Bar.

During Friday and Saturday the Bar was still impassable; and I was pleased to have a fair opportunity of seeing the outside of it and the coast-line at a time when the Bar was pronounced to be in a worse state than it had been in for many years.

The line of coast to the northward of Port Natal lies nearly N.E. and S.W. Along this coast-line the gulf stream sets about S.W., at a rate of from one mile and a half to four miles per hour, according as the stream is retarded or accelerated by the wind.

When the wind is anything to the southward of east, the southern terminus of the entrance of the harbour, which is a steep bluff, about a mile in extent, and running to the N.E., in a line nearly with the coast, effectually shelters the harbour; and the Bar at the entrance, having from eight to eleven feet of water on it, is passable, and the sea at such times does not break on the Bar.

As the wind draws more to the southward, it meets with the usual set of the current, and deflects it to the eastward from the mouth of the harbour, so that any detritus in solution is not at such times deposited at the mouth of the harbour.

On the other hand, when the wind is in that quarter of the compass from north to east, which it frequently is at Natal, the wind increases the velocity of the current, sometimes to as much as four miles per hour, and this accelerated current, setting down the coast, is arrested by the Bluff already referred to. The consequence is, that to the northward of this Bluff—which is the direct entrance into the harbour—all the detritus in solution, carried down by the stream, is deposited there; and, as the current passes along a sandy shore immediately before arriving at the Bluff, a great deposit of sand is the natural consequence; and the filling up of the entrance of the harbour of Port Natal would be the result. This is prevented by the scoure which takes place on the ebbing of the tide, augmented by the water of the river Umlas, which runs into Port Natal.

On the northern shore of the entrance of the harbour a pier has been commenced, extending seawards, and running somewhat parallel with the opposite shore of the entrance, which is the inner side of the Bluff. The object of this pier is to confine the channel, by which means it is hoped to increase the power of the scourage, and, with the assistance of a steam dredge, to keep the Bar clear; so as to have on it at all times twelve feet of water, while at high tides it is expected that there will be twenty-two feet.

At the time of our visit, Mr. Pilkington, the Engineer of the Cape colony, and Mr. Skeade, R.N., an able marine surveyor, were at Natal, examining the Bar and Harbour. What the nature of their report has been I do not know; but with the harbour before me, and the best admiralty chart, I came to the conclusion that to make Port Natal what it ought to be, the following plan should be adopted :—

From Fort Farewell, in a line with the pier now building, run out a breakwater into four fathoms of water to the eastward, until in a line with the eastern extreme of the Bluff, after which, curve the breakwater to the southward and eastward, and continue the Bluff, by means of a similar pier, leaving a sufficient opening for vessels under canvas to enter in foul weather. This would form a large horse-shoe Harbour of Refuge outside of the Bar, having at its entrance, which should face the south-east, from five to six fathoms of water.

Increase the scoure in Port Natal harbour, by leading into it the river Umgani in addition to the Umlas, and not only would twenty-two feet of water be found on the Bar, but in the course of time the sand now forming the Bar would be washed away and the Bar would entirely disappear, and the Breakwater to the northward would prevent its ever forming again.

The expense of such an undertaking would be considerable; but the loss and damage sustained by shipping, at present, for want of a harbour, is more than the interest of a sum which would easily cover that expense; while the increased revenue from the formation of such a harbour would soon enable the colony to liquidate any liability incurred for so desirable an end.

The southern pier, from the bluff, might be built of the bluff itself; which is stone of a quality durable but not difficult to work. While the northern pier, forming the breakwater, might be constructed of timber and stone. How quickly, easily, and permanently such a breakwater might be formed, may be learned from the wharves running out into the River St. Lawrence, at Point Levi, opposite to the city of Quebec.

These wharves are built in compartments of hard durable timber. The timber compartments are floated out, and placed over the spot where they are intended to be built in, and they have planks secured in them, forming a rough bottom. The compartment is put in position by loading it with stones, when it gradually sinks to its proper place; it is then loaded with more stones, until permanently fixed. Another compartment is similarly placed, on top of the former, and piers are thus run out into forty feet of water. All these compartments are firmly secured to each other by strong logs of timber at the top, the sides, and transversely.

These piers form docks or basins along the

bank of the St. Lawrence, under the shelter of, and attached to which, ships of the largest tonnage lie in security at all times, in a river with a great rise and fall, having a current with a considerable velocity. When the ice in Upper Canada breaks up, and floats down the St. Lawrence, packing up mountain on mountain of ice, and crumpling up steamers and vessels in the stream as if they were made of paper, the ships lying under shelter of the piers described escape all danger. The stream of the St. Lawrence, carrying on its bosom the materials for forming icebergs, makes no more impression on these than on the solid rock.

In proposing to build the northern pier of timber and stone combined, the objects considered have been :—Firstly, economy, which is everything in great undertakings of this nature, especially when connected with a young colony. Secondly, expedition, for the rapid development of the resources of Natal is crushed by the want of a harbour. Thirdly, the timber required for such an undertaking is to be found on the third terrace of the colony, at a distance of from forty to sixty miles from the harbour ; while procuring which, roads would have to be made, thereby providing the greatest internal want of the colony.

The people of D'Urban have already undertaken the construction of a railway from the pier now forming to D'Urban, a distance of two or more miles, and the formation of the proposed Breakwater would cause that railway to be extended along the fertile sugar, coffee, and indigo producing valleys, to the timber districts.

I have already alluded to Captain Veitch, R.E., F.R.S., the intelligent engineer to the Board of Admiralty, as the officer who planned the Harbour of Refuge at Table Bay. Since my return to England, that gentleman has done me the honour of consulting me relative to Natal harbour, and the foregoing is the substance of my communication to him. I have reason to believe that a plan, similar to that proposed by me, is now under consideration.

Sunday, the 5th of July, the bar being practicable, Mrs. M'Leod, her maid, who was an old resident at Natal, Captain Gordon, and myself, landed in the port boat at about two P.M. Being high water, by means of a small boat we were able to ascend a creek in the harbour, leading to the house of Mr. Cato, Vice-Consul for America, Sweden, Norway, &c., and, after making the acquaintance of Mr. and Mrs. Cato, we proceeded, on foot, to Weeden's (late M'Donald's) Hotel, where we were made very comfortable during our visit to D'Urban.

There were a number of small vessels in the harbour, and some of a larger tonnage than I was prepared to meet with; but I was told that the latter took advantage of the Bar at certain times, about once a fortnight, when there were 15 feet of water on it.

The Harbour of Port Natal is a vast circular pond (for, from its security, I can call it nothing else), three miles in depth, and having a breadth of about one mile and a half. In it there are three islands, easy of access at low water; and the Harbour could contain, at present, about thirty vessels, sheltered from every point of the compass. When the Harbour of Refuge, outside of the Bar, is constructed, it requires no prophetic powers to foretell the future of this port. The three islands will form the foundations of large warehouses, holding the imports and exports of the colony, and of the neighbouring Orange Free State, which has no other outlet for its commerce. The creeks, running between these three islands, will form floating-docks; while, on the sides of this extensive harbour, dry docks for repairing, and building-yards for constructing, ships, will find their natural locations. Viewing this harbour with reference to the wants of the country, there is no doubt that it will become the Liverpool of South-Eastern Africa; but when we reflect that between Europe and India, by way of the Cape of Good Hope, there is only one dry dock to repair disabled ships, and that only at Port Louis, Mauritius, in the region of hurricanes, which all are anxious to avoid, it may readily be imagined what numbers of ships will be attracted to Port Natal with its Harbour of Refuge and dry docks. Many vessels disabled by the hurricane, now obliged to put into Mauritius, however distant from it they may be, will resort to Natal, where the gulf stream, setting along South Eastern Africa, will aid them to reach this haven of safety.

The town of D'Urban is situated on this fine harbour, and is about a mile distant ftom the anchorage.

It is of recent construction, well laid out, the streets very wide, and lined with beautiful trees, which give to it a charmingly healthy and cheerful appearance. The houses are about 400 in number, built principally of wood, but giving place to stone edifices. It contains about 1,200 Europeans, mostly English, who have their Episcopalian Church and Wesleyan Methodist Chapel.

About twenty miles from Port Natal, Verulam is situated, at present a small town, but, from its being in the centre of the district where sugar, arrowroot, and indigo are grown, and from its position on the right bank of the Umbloti River, it must soon become a place of importance, although it has sprung into existence since 1850.

The capital of the colony is Pieter-Maritzburg, sometimes already abbreviated to Maritzburg, and is called after one of the martyred Dutch farmers who founded the colony, with the early history of which he is inseparably connected. It is the see of a bishop, the first of whom is the well-known author of Colenso's "Ten Weeks in Natal." It stands on the second terrace of the colony, is well watered, and built in the Dutch style. It is the seat of government, and contains about 1,800 Europeans.

On coming from the ship in the port boat, we heard some statements relative to a suspicious vessel seen off the port some days previous to our arrival, and which, it appears, must have slipped away just about the time we were directing our course towards the harbour.

Immediately we reached the shore, we made some inquiries about this vessel, and learned as follows:—

It appears that, on the Monday previous to our arrival, a vessel approached Port Natal and anchored far out. This vessel had been seen for two days from the signal-house on the Bluff, and the day before she anchored off the harbour, she was at anchor for some hours off the mouth of the

Umlazi River, which is eight miles from Port Natal. She was believed from her build—long, low, and rakish—to be the "Jessie Macfarlane," an iron barque, under English colours, which was expected about that time from the Cape of Good Hope.

Soon after the stranger anchored, she was boarded by the port boat, and the captain of her, who spoke English, said that he was in want of water and refreshments, that he had a cargo of rum, and was bound from Havannah to Madagascar. The vessel appeared to be very light, and some of the crew said that she was in ballast. On the Coxswain of the port boat remarking that the vessel had a large crew, the Captain replied that he had been fortunate in picking up the crew of a vessel, who had abandoned their ship when she was sinking.

The crew of the port boat were permitted to ascend her side; and the pilot who went to her in the port boat had some questions put to him which made the Natalians acquainted with the voyage upon which the stranger was bound.

It appears that a boat, with six men in her, had

left the vessel on the previous evening, when off the Umlazi, and the captain of the Slaver was anxious to know if they would succeed in attaining the object they had gone in search of, namely, the purchase of a cargo of the natives.

No sooner was this question put to the pilot, than he became greatly alarmed; the chest lying open on the deck of the stranger immediately came to his remembrance; glancing round the cabin, he observed it full of arms, in good condition; and, hurrying on deck, he observed preparations making for placing guns in the port-holes, with which the vessel was pierced.

The pilot, unfortunately for the cause of humanity, instead of using a *ruse* to entrap the man-stealer, thought only of his personal safety, and therefore stated that there was a British sloop of war in the Harbour of Natal. This was enough to alarm the Slaver; the port boat was immediately ordered off; the sails were let fall from the topsails yards, which had been at the mast head during the whole time that she remained at anchor; and while the topsails were being sheeted home, the small warp with which she had brought up was slipped, and, two minutes after hearing that Natal was a British colony, and that there was a vessel of war at anchor there, the stranger was off to the northward.

The port boat had hardly arrived in the harbour with the astounding intelligence that there had been a large slaver at anchor off the port, endeavouring to obtain some of the natives by purchase, when six Spaniards made their appearance in D'Urban.

On the morning of the following day, Tuesday, they were examined relative to the stranger. They denied all knowledge of the vessel being a slaver, but said that they shipped at Havannah on the 5th of April, the day she sailed; that they never signed or saw any articles; that they never saw the hold of the vessel, the hatches having been battened down during the whole voyage; that the Captain was an American, and the vessel a large three-masted American clipper; that they were not acquainted with the name of the Captain, nor that of the owners of the vessel; and that even the name of the vessel was unknown to them. They declared themselves to be all Spaniards; that they had been sent on shore with twenty-eight dollars, to buy provisions; and that, when landing at the mouth of the Umlazi, their boat was capsized, and with difficulty they reached the shore. They further stated that, when the Captain saw the boat was swamped, he approached the surf in another boat, and directed them to walk round to Natal, and stated that he would call for them there.

The magistrate ordered them rations and lodgings, as shipwrecked seamen, and directed the Mate to see to their good behaviour, until they could be forwarded to the Cape.

When the Mate really found that the Slaver had gone, and that there was no hope of her return, he communicated the fact that the vessel was a Slaver in ballast, from Havannah, bound to Cape Corrientes for a cargo of slaves; and having on board 70,000 dollars for the purchase of her cargo. It appears that the Captain was an American, of the name of John Ward, and that the vessel's name was the "Minnetonka." The Mate, who was a Spaniard, and the Captain had a quarrel on the passage, and the former imagined that landing him in the Umlazi was a trick to get rid of him.

By degrees it was learned that twenty-one slavers had been towed out of the Havannah, in open day, during the space of one month. These vessels left Cuba openly, with the declared intention of proceeding to Africa for cargoes of slaves. Fourteen of these vessels were going to make a run to the West Coast; and the remaining seven, being larger, were going to the East Coast, to obtain their cargoes in the Mozambique Channel, where the Emperor of the French had established the Slave Trade, under the denomination of Free Labour Emigration.

It will hereafter be shown that, by following the motions of this Slave barque "Minnetonka," under both American and Spanish colours—for Captain Ward used both flags whenever it suited his convenience—I discovered the Slave Trade carried on by the Portuguese authorities in the Province of Mozambique, from Cape Delgado to Delagoa Bay; and was further enabled to drag to light, and lay before the world, the whole system of French free-labour emigration, as carried on by delegated authority;—a system of so-called emigration, which has caused a renewal of all the horrors perpetrated by the natives on each other, for the purpose of supplying that Slave Trade which England has, for more than half a century, been endeavouring to put an end to by a lavish expenditure of money, and the continued sacrifice of the most heroic spirits in her peerless Navy.

In confirmation of the statement of the Mate of the "Minnetonka," that she was bound for Cape Corrientes, I learned at Natal that four full cargoes of Africans had been shipped from that locality within the two last months, while Her Majesty's Consul for Mozambique was detained at the Cape of Good Hope; and the Mozambique Channel was left without a cruiser on the advice of Mr. Joăo de Costa Soares, better known as "John of the Coast;"—the governor of Inhambane and "John of the Coast's" aunt supplying the slaves for those four vessels.

On the morning after landing at D'Urban, a deputation from the Chamber of Commerce of Natal did me the honour of waiting on me at Weeden's Hotel, to lay before me the great difficulties which the Natal merchants had to encounter in pushing British commerce into Eastern Africa. They stated that the rates of duty charged by the Portuguese authorities were too high, and at least fifty per cent. above the tariff established by the government at Lisbon; that every conceivable difficulty was thrown in the way of legal traders, and that it was impossible to carry on legitimate commerce in those parts possessed by the Portuguese; while, on every other part of the coast, between Cape Delgado and Delagoa Bay, which did not belong to the Portuguese, they were forbidden to trade with the natives, under pain of their property being confiscated.

To this I replied:—"That the object of Her Majesty's government in appointing a Consul to Mozambique was to establish Legitimate Trade in those parts, and at the same time to abolish the Slave Trade; and that it would be my most earnest endeavour to establish commercial relations on those terms which ought to subsist between the subjects of friendly sovereigns."

A member of the deputation next inquired if I

could not promote the supply of Native Labour from Mozambique to Natal, placing this British Colony on the same terms, as to labour, as the neighbouring French Colony of Reunion.

To this I replied :—" That if an application of that nature was made to the Lieutenant-governor of the Colony, no doubt it would receive an immediate and definite reply."

Hereupon the deputation withdrew; and Captain Gordon and myself had a good laugh at the proposal of one member of the deputation to make Her Majesty's Consul a Delegate for obtaining free labour from Mozambique.

During the course of that morning I had a visit from Mr. G. W. Duncan, who had been up to Delagoa Bay, in a small Cutter called the "Herald," of Natal, endeavouring to establish commercial relations with the natives on the south part of that Bay, which is British territory; and he complained to me of the obstacles thrown in his way by the Portuguese authorities at Lourenço Marques, situated in that Bay, in preventing him from trading with persons who were willing to do so; and also of their preventing him trading with the Zulus in the British territory on the south part of Delagoa Bay, unless he first paid duties to the custom-house at Lourenço Marques. To give me some further insight into the conduct of the authorities at the above-named place, he placed in my hands a copy of the following letter, which will be again referred to in these pages:—

"DELAGOA BAY AND THE SLAVE TRADE ON THE EAST AFRICAN COAST.

"To the Editor of the *Natal Mercury*.

"SIR,

"During my stay at Lourenço Marques, Delagoa Bay, I usually visited, after business hours, persons there considered of high standing; and, being in quest of knowledge that might in future prove advantageous, I generally introduced such subjects as would best lead to the information I was most desirous of gaining.

"Their commercial policy is not to deal in trifles. Specimens illustrative of natural history, which excite the admiration of the civilized portion of the world, have with them no charm.

Ivory and Negroes appear to be the only articles of commerce to which they aspire, and they succeed in obtaining them to an astonishing extent, at comparatively small cost.

"With regard to ivory, each merchant has several negro hunte[illegible] kill a number of elephants during th[illegible]des which they purchase ivory [illegible]he banks of the Manakusi, or [illegible] River, which river offers grea[illegible] being navigable for craft of l[illegible]

"Th[illegible]polized by the Portuguese, who [illegible] foreigners to penetrate. In pr[illegible] mention that, having a strong [illegible]as many discoveries as I could, for [illegible]ent of trade and commerce, I intimated [illegible]e authorities my intention of entering [illegible] river, but was forbidden to do so, with a[illegible]nest caution as to the consequence, which, I was told, would be the seizure of the cutter and cargo; that, though their jurisdiction did not extend so far, yet I should expose myself, if I attempted the passage of the river, both in going in and in coming out.

"But there are, doubtless, other motives than those of monopoly in the ivory trade, which I will leave your readers to conjecture from the following information which I gathered as to the manner in which the abominable practice of slave dealing is carried on.

"It does not unfrequently happen that irruptions take place between neighbouring tribes, with a view to the number of prisoners they may be fortunate in taking, as a means of obtaining articles of home consumption, such as beads, blankets, &c., which are obtained in exchange for the unfortunate captives. Those of the age of eighteen years are most suitable; all above that age, I was told, are put to death. The women are distributed among the conquering warriors, and the young men sold into slavery. Slaves in any number can thus be procured; the only difficulty traders have to contend with is to secure them; and, happily, that difficulty does exist, else, I imagine, it would be beyond human power to depict the misery which would ensue.

"In spite of all difficulties, however, the trade is carried on with comparative impunity, and with considerable success. Agents are established on the East Coast of Africa, by slave merchants, to purchase slaves of those who obtain them in barter. Those agents act under instructions, particularly as to signs, and signals, and places of embarkation; and also establish relations with those already engaged in the traffic, from whom and through whom large numbers of negroes are collected, and chained in small groups, some by the neck, and others by the hand, and are then marched, at the time, and to the place appointed, to await the arrival of the vessel that is to carry them to their destiny.

"A trial was made, not long since, to establish a 'legitimate' trade, if in any way it can be called legitimate. Not many months ago, four or five vessels, carrying the French flag, called at Killimane, for the purpose of establishing a Free Emigration.

"Negotiations were entered into between the Governor and the Agent. The former, it was said, was well 'palmed,' and offered opportunity to all large slaveholders to supply the agent with a large number of so-called 'free emigrants.' The system upon which it was carried out, I am told, was similar to that which is practised for procuring coolies, with this difference, that the Africans were purchased and sold into hopeless bondage. The truth of this statement can easily be ascertained by a reference to the Cabinet at Lisbon, under whose notice, I learned, the affair has been brought. Such an atrocity, practised almost within call of a British port, is horrible to contemplate, more especially when there is safe anchorage at this port for a man-of-war cruiser; besides which, from what I learn, the south side of Delagoa Bay, having been ceded to the British Government, can be made available, not only for the suppression of slavery, but for the advancement of trade and commerce. It is to all appearance very desirable, and no doubt very fertile, as considerable traffic is carried on between the Portuguese and the queen of the island, who is a tributary of our Zulu neighbour, Panda.

"Direct slavery is not countenanced by the Portuguese authorities. So far they act in union with their government; but it is my belief, from information gathered, that they aid and abet all concerned in it.

"It is well known that the government of Delagoa have taken negro prisoners, and sold them to persons residing in the town. Moreover, almost all Moorish sloops, trading between Delagoa Bay and the Mozambique, are slavers in a modified form. Limited numbers of slaves are occasionally shipped on board of them, to and from Mozambique, with passports as passengers, to evade detection if overhauled by a cruiser.

"Considering, sir, your space valuable, I have much curtailed this subject. I could, by dwelling lengthily upon it, have established beyond a doubt the certainty of slave-trading on this coast; but forbear, hoping that you will pardon me for having already encroached at great length, and that what I have said will be sufficient to awaken those whose duty it is to notice such startling facts; and to endeavour, by all possible means, to put an end to these appalling outrages upon our common humanity.—I am, sir, your obedient servant,

"G. W. Duncan.

"D'Urban, June, 1857."

The information obtained at Port Natal, relative to slaving carried on in the Mozambique Channel, induced Captain Gordon and myself to hasten our movements, and, by the time the deputation had retired, our party were ready to return to the harbour.

The tide being out, we proceeded along the margin of the bay in the usual conveyance employed in this colony. It consisted of a large lumbering four-wheeled waggon, drawn by eight oxen. In the waggon, chairs were placed to sit upon; and it was driven by a Zulu Kaffir, who flourished a long whip, with which at one moment he would tickle the ear of one of the leaders, and then, in quick succession, distribute his favours on the remainder of the team in such a way as to drive them furious. This Kaffir was a good type of his class, his hair being done up in the "married men style." On a Kaffir being married, it is usual for the wife to do up the hair of her lord and master in the following manner:—A ring fitting tight on the top of the head is provided; sometimes the ring is made of iron, occasionally of brass, but more generally of some elastic climber. The hair is drawn up over this ring, and retained in its place by gum from the mimosa, or any glutinous matter. In the course of time it becomes as hard as iron, and will resist, not only a severe blow, but the rays of an African sun, affording a protection against fever and the tomahawk.

Our Kaffir Jehu had a name for every one of his oxen. He appeared to be particularly down upon "Sir Harry Smith," while "Sir George Grey" was a prime favourite. Occasionally the Kaffir would stand up, and after flourishing his whip in the air, accompanied with, to us, unintelligible jargon, he would come down with terrific violence on "Aliwal," and then make a furious dig with the handle of his whip at "Sobraon," who was one of the wheelers. All went pretty well until we came nearly to the end of the journey, when "Sir George Grey," who up to this time had been deservedly, from the way in which he worked, a great favourite, happened to stumble. Down jumped the Kaffir, and laid into poor "Sir George Grey" with as much reason and sense of justice as if he had been a Colonial Minister.

After our party were seated in the port boat,

an extraordinary looking individual, with a profusion of red locks on his head, making one quite warm to look at him, presented me with a small note, requesting that "His Excellency would settle that small account before he left the harbour." On opening the note, I found it was a formal document demanding the small amount of three pounds, five shillings, for the use of the small boat which had taken us up the creek on the previous day, after getting out of the port boat. This, of course, I refused to pay, especially as I had given what I considered a sufficient amount to the two men who had rowed us up the creek. I found the stranger was called "Daft Jemmy," and that he obtained a living in this manner by imposing upon all persons arriving at Port Natal. I informed him that I had no intention of paying for a boat twice, and told the port boat to shove off. Nothing daunted, "Daft Jemmy" hailed the coxswain to "accept any amount which 'His Excellency' might think proper to offer, on account, as no doubt he would settle the balance next time he came to Natal."

We crossed the bar in safety; reached the "Hermes;" and I closed my dispatches for England, and wrote to the Admiral and Mr. Frere, urging them to send all the disposable steam force up the Mozambique Channel for the purpose of seizing vessels carrying on the slave trade in those waters. These matters being finished, Captain Gordon started in chase of the "Minnetonka," now supposed to be about loading her cargo of slaves.

CHAPTER VII.

Present State of Natal—Physical Formation—Succession of Terraces—Products most suitable for Each—Labour Required for Natal—Development and Prosperity of Free Labour Colonies—The Destruction of the Slave Trade—Climate of Natal—"Shall we Retain our Colonies?"

WHILE the "Hermes" is steaming away to the Northward in search of the "Minnetonka," we purpose giving to the reader a short statement of the present condition of the Colony of Natal.

A history of Natal has already been written by the Rev. Mr. Holden, which, combined with Five Lectures on Natal by the Hon. Henry Cloete, LL.D., the celebrated Recorder of Natal, and the perusal of "Ten Weeks in Natal" by Bishop Colenso, will give those anxious to obtain definite information relative to the origin, rise, and rapid progress of this colony, a very fair insight into its state previous to the era of self-government. It is hoped that the following statement, together with the observations contained in the last chapter relative to the harbour of Port Natal, may be acceptable to those seeking information relative to the colony up to the present date.

The British Colony of Natal, situated on the south-east coast of Africa, extends from latitude 29°16′ to latitude 31° 34′ south; or, speaking more definitely, from the mouth of the river Omzinyat, or Fisher's River, to that of the Umzimkulu, which latter river divides it from the rich district of Kaffraria. It will thus be seen that it has a coast line of 150 miles, washed by the Indian Ocean, and along which the gulf stream runs to the south west, at a velocity of from one and a-half to four miles per hour. From the coast it extends into the country a distance of eighty miles to the Quathlamba Mountains, which divide it from the neighbouring Boer Settlement, called the Orange Free State. It has an area of 18,000 square miles, or about one-third of that of England and Wales. Viewed, as to its territorial extent, with other colonies of Great Britain, it holds a very insignificant position; but its physical formation is such that, small though it may be, it is capable of producing the luxuriant vegetation of the tropics in close proximity with that of the more temperate climate of Europe; —forming a *bijou* in South Eastern Africa, which must have a considerable effect in civilizing the natives of the surrounding territories.

The variety in the soil and climate of this interesting and truly valuable possession of Great Britain is caused by the country rising rapidly from the Indian Ocean in a succession of four steps or terraces, each having an average width of twenty miles, with its own peculiarity of soil and climate.

Along the lower terrace, which is washed by the Indian Ocean, the heat is greatest; and though scarcely even in the height of the hot season to be called "tropical," outside of which the colony lies, yet it is sufficient to allow of the growth of cotton, sugar, coffee, indigo, arrowroot, pine-apples, bananas, and the cocoa-nut, and oil palms (as soon as introduced), over an area of three thousand square miles. In addition to which, the coast line being washed by the gulf stream, the moist warm temperature from which, aided by the saline breezes from the ocean, render a belt of this coast line, extending from high water mark to five or ten miles inland, peculiarly adapted for the growth of the sea-island cotton, whose long fleecy staple is the produce of similar physical advantages. This fact alone will show the value of the lower or sea-coast terrace of the Colony of Natal; upwards of 1000 square miles of which are capable of producing the most highly prized of the cottons of America, without the accompanying drawback of an unhealthy climate for the European constitution.

In this region, where vegetation is luxuriant, there is much woodland and park-like scenery, which gradually disappears as one proceeds inland, while the temperature is diminished, and the air becomes clear and bracing.

The second terrace of the colony is almost bare of trees; but well adapted for grazing purposes. It affords abundant crops of hay, oat fodder, mealies, or Indian corn and barley.

The third terrace contains plenty of forest timber of considerable size and of very superior quality, both for the wants of the colony and for ship-building purposes.

The fourth terrace is well adapted for growing wheat and all European productions.

Throughout the length and breadth of the colony it is well watered, there being a stream every four or five miles of its extent. These streams are never dried up, excepting some few of them in the winter season, when the temperature, even along the coast, is delightfully cool and pleasant. During this season, which lasts for four or five months, more inland there is hoar frost upon the ground, and sometimes snow upon the wooded highlands; while on the Quathlamba Mountains it may be seen for a week or ten days together.

Products of Natal—

Cotton. The seed named the "petit gulf prolific," is said to be the most successful yet tried at Natal. One pound weight of this seed, which costs ten shillings, is sufficient to plant an acre of ground. September, October, and November are the months for planting it. The yield of one acre, having 6,000 plants on it, averaged two and a half pounds of seed cotton per plant, which, when reduced by the cotton cleaning gin, gave one pound and one quarter of clean cotton per plant; at sixpence per pound this would give the enormous return of 187*l.* 10*s.* sterling per acre. There are, at the lowest computation, 640,000 acres, on the lower or coast line terrace of the colony, which will produce cotton of this quality, so that our Liverpool merchants may look forward to a supply of no less than 4,800,000,000 lbs. of cotton from one of the smallest and latest acquired of our colonies. Surely a colony, whose capability for producing one of the great staples of our manufactures is thus shown to be almost unlimited, deserves the most encouraging attention of our statesmen both in a commercial and anti-slavery light.

Wool. This article may be produced as well as in the Cape of Good Hope, although for some time it was believed that the grass, being too rank and abundant, either killed the sheep or filled the wool with seeds and weeds. As cultivation increases, the annoying insects, which did much destruction to the sheep and cattle by living upon and impoverishing them, are rapidly disappearing. Some parts of the colony, where horses and cattle would not thrive, are now well known as breeding districts, and the colonists have commenced exporting both cattle and horses, to some considerable extent, to the island of Mauritius.

Sugar. The sugar-cane flourishes here remarkably well; and, from the great abundance of water, the cane is not likely to be attacked by the insect called the "borer," which does so much destruction at Mauritius.

There are already in the colony seven sugar mills, some of considerable power. Large portions of the country are being planted with the cane, and it is said that this virgin soil yields from three to four tons of sugar per acre.

The supply at present is not great, as the colonists are hampered for want of labour, more especially that labour adapted for the sugar-cane, which appears to be found in Indian or Chinese coolie labour. As soon as facilities are afforded to the colony of Natal for coolie labour, similar to that employed at Mauritius, the yield of this article alone will be enormous; there being at least 1,280,000 acres of the soil, irrespective of what may be more appropriately devoted to cotton, capable of producing sugar. It may be confidently asserted that the supply of Natal sugar will not equal the demand. Its saccharine properties have been proved by Mr. Milne, the great sugar-refiner at Bristol, to be stronger than the Mauritius sugar, and not surpassed by the best Trinidad. Already, from the balcony of one house, no less than seven shafts can be seen puffing away the fumes of boiling syrup; and, when labour is supplied to Natal, this necessary for the artisan of the mother country will be supplied at a much reduced price, completely driving slave-grown sugar out of the market. The growing of mealies, or Indian corn, may be carried on at the same time as that of sugar. The mealies ought to be grown in every other row of the cane, and about twice the distance apart of the cane roots. By this means the young canes are protected, and provision is made for the labourers without impoverishing the ground or materially increasing the labour of the cane-fields.

Indigo. Many varieties of indigo grow luxuriantly and wild in the colony; almost justifying the thought that on this side of Africa the plant is indigenous, although we are aware that on the west coast it was introduced by the Jesuits, and perhaps also, by way of the Zambesi, into the interior.

Large factories are being erected for the manufacture of indigo; and, in order that it may be thoroughly successful, arrangements have been made for the introduction of persons who have been already acquainted with its manufacture in the island of Java.

Tobacco. The cultivation of tobacco has been carried on for some considerable time, but on a very small scale, in consequence of the want of labour. Two crops may be grown in the year; and there is an ample market for it already in the colony, which imports annually thousands of pounds weight of the real Virginia.

On the higher terraces inland, to a great extent, wheat, oats, barley, and other cereals are grown; while the climate of those districts admirably suits them for the pasturage and rearing of sheep and cattle, with which they may be said already to abound.

The export of wool, from the neighbouring Boer Settlement of the Orange Free State, through Natal, is increasing rapidly, while the enterprise of the young Natalians has given them access to the ivory grounds of the Zulus, who prefer dealing with them rather than with the Transvaal Republic Boers.

Coffee and Arrowroot. The following testimony to the quality of Natal coffee and arrowroot was forwarded last year to Natal :—

"3, King William Street, London, E.C.
"September 17, 1858.

"Gentlemen,

"We have carefully tested the two samples of Natal coffee you sent us. We find the Costa Rica kind very strong coffee, and worth, in our present market, 65*s.* to 68*s.* per cwt., in bond. The sample of West India kind is strong, rich, good coffee, full of aroma, and worth about 70*s.* to 75*s.* in bond. If such coffees are sent to England, we think they will always command good market value, as does your Natal arrowroot, &c., &c.

"PHILLIPS AND CO.

"Messrs. Savory, Natal."

Large quantities of American flour, and even the coarser description of that produced at the Cape, are imported into Natal; but now that farmers are turning their attention to the production of wheat, which will flourish on the upper terraces, we may expect to see bread stuffs cheaper; more especially as numbers of the Boers, getting disgusted with the unsettled aspect of affairs in the two neighbouring Boer states, are coming from beyond the Drakenburg Mountains, and settling themselves down on the higher terraces of Natal, from which great quantities of wheat and cattle may soon be expected, not only for the supply of cheap and abundant food for the colonists, but for the purposes of exportation.

I have already touched upon the subject of labour, and stated that the labour adapted for the cultivation of the soil is greatly required at Natal. Looking at a chart of the country, one would exclaim, how can this possibly be the case when the colony of Natal is surrounded on all sides, but that facing the ocean, with countries abounding in natives? Yes; but natives unadapted for the wants of the soil. The Zulus are a pastoral people, and, as long as employed in tending cattle, they are very well; but, as yet, they have shown no aptitude for agricultural purposes—such occupation is contrary to their nature, and to the customs of their ancestors, who have always been a nomadic race.

With difficulty the colonists of Natal can secure the services of a native, even in household work, for more than six months at a time. At the end of that period, the Zulu Kaffir wishes to return to his own people, to enjoy the sweets of liberty in the forest, or the boundless prairie, to drink of the milk of his own krall, and dance with the Kaffir girls. This is all very natural; and it depends greatly on the treatment which he has received from the white man if he will ever return. In some instances, when pleased with his situation, a Kaffir, previous to the time of leaving, will ask his employer permission to bring his little brother, for the purpose of teaching him the work of the place. If his application is acceded to, the Kaffir will take great trouble to teach his younger brother what he is required to do in order to give satisfaction to his employer. When the senior's period of engagement has expired, his brother fills his place for another six months, and then he is succeeded by some other member of his family, whom he has prepared. In this manner, the situation, when a good one, is kept in a family; and the colonists, knowing this, are anxious to get hold of what is called a "nest of Kaffirs"—that is, where there are a number in a family—for by that means they are provided at all times with domestic labour, and generally well served. But the Kaffir, who will clean windows, and wash plates and glasses very carefully, will not labour in the field. Harder working Kaffirs—and there are some few—when they have passed through the school of industrial training, and have learned their own value, like many other men having similar souls, but different coloured skins, will obtain credit for a waggon and oxen, and throw their labour into the market in a different form from their less industrious brethren.

Natal wants labour, and of a description which can only be supplied from India; the native of which, having for ages cultivated the soil, has an aptitude for this description of labour, in which he displays a degree of neatness which cannot be found among the nomadic pastoral races of Africa.

Coolie labour must, therefore, be provided either from India or from China: let it be abundant, and hampered with no regulation which is not for the protection of the labourer. By restricting the supply of labour to our colonies, obstacles are placed in the way of their development which prevent them so successfully competing with the Slave Labour States of America and Cuba as they otherwise might do. On the other hand, by supplying abundance of labour, our colonies will produce supplies for European markets in so great abundance, and at such a great reduction in cost, that the working men of our own country will be able to obtain in plenty many articles which are now looked upon almost as luxuries, although absolutely necessaries to overworked frames; while, at the same time, the produce of slave labour, being so much dearer, will find no market, and the producing article, namely, slave labour, must entirely cease.

With reference to the climate of Natal, besides what has here been stated, it is only necessary to add the testimony of my late lamented friend, Dr. Stranger, who, after surviving the unfortunate "Niger Expedition" of 1841, died at Natal, while filling the important post of Surveyor General of that Colony. The worthy doctor's report states:—

"The climate of Natal is very healthy, but, I think, more salubrious at some distance from the coast. There appears to be scarcely any disease incidental to the country. Dysentery is not frequent; ophthalmia occurs occasionally, and is, perhaps, the only disease of the colony; it is, however, not often of a severe character.

"The rains commence with violent thunderstorms about the month of September, and continue till about April, when they terminate with thunder. During the rainy season, which is also the summer, the average daily temperature is about 76°, but the evenings are generally cooled by a

S.E. breeze. The thermometer rarely rises above 80°. The winter temperature varies from 50° to 60°; frosts are frequent in the higher parts of the district, and at the Mooi River, in June, I have seen the thermometer stand at 27° at 7 A.M. Cold nights are generally succeeded by warm days. Rain rarely falls in the interior between or during the months of May and August. On the coast the seasons are not so well defined, as showers occur throughout the year. Long droughts are almost unknown."

To Natal has been accorded by the Imperial government the great boon of Self-government; and while taking leave of this Colony, before we proceed to the northward, and view the state of other settlements which are not under the ameliorating influence of British rule, it may not be inappropriate to quote a few words from an article in the *Edinburgh Review*, of April, 1850, headed, "Shall we retain our Colonies." The words referred to are:—

"The affection of the colonists it is easy to preserve, or to recover, where, through misjudgment or misunderstanding, it has been shaken or impaired. By ruling them with forbearance, steadiness, and justice; by leading them forward in the path of freedom with an encouraging but cautious hand; by bestowing upon them the fullest powers of Self-government, wherever the influence of British blood is large enough to warrant such a course; in a word, by following out the line of policy announced and defended by Lord John Russel, in his speech on the introduction of a Bill for the government of the Australian colonies, in February of the last year, we may secure the existence and rivet the cohesion of a dominion blest with the wisest, soberest, most beneficial form of liberty which the world has yet enjoyed, and spreading to distant lands and future ages the highest, most prolific, and most expansive development of civilization which Providence has ever granted to humanity."

CHAPTER VIII.

Port St. Lucia—Zulu Country—Panda—Delagoa Bay—Its Unhealthiness; Causes Examined—Lourenço Marques—Dutch Fort—Tembe and Iniack—British Territory—Fecundity of Boer Females—Products—Transvaal Republic—Mineral Wealth—Future of the Country.

After leaving the limits of the Colony of Natal, in proceeding to the northward, the first port which attracts attention is that of Port St. Lucia, in latitude 28° 26′ S., and longitude 32° 26′ E.

This port is admirably adapted for throwing supplies of ammunition, and also useful commodities, into the Zulu country, from which they are carried into the Orange Free State, and the Transvaal Republic, thereby eluding the custom's dues payable at the Cape of Good Hope and Natal.

A considerable trade of this description is already established by several mercantile houses at the Cape of Good Hope; and, this fact having become known in London and Liverpool, merchants are naturally inquiring what articles of trade are suitable for a port where no duties whatever are levied, and where the returns of ivory, hides, horns, and hoofs are immediate.*

As the colony of the Cape of Good Hope pays annually to the Boers 5,000*l.* (five thousand pounds sterling) as a compensation for the duties levied on commodities passing through that colony to the Orange Free State and Transvaal Republic, it is natural to expect that the revenue of that colony should be protected by obtaining possession of a port at present belonging to no country, and which offers a sore temptation to the Boers, ever on the look-out for an outlet for their productions, without passing through and

* The author will be happy to supply a list of articles suited for a cargo which will find a ready market along the E. Coast of Africa.

enriching a country from which they *trecked*, in consequence of real or imagined wrongs.

From Port St. Lucia, proceeding northwards, we pass a line of coast, of which we absolutely know nothing, until we arrive at Cape Colatto, in latitude 26° 4′ S., and longitude 33° 1′ E.

The whole of this coast is low, and washed by the gulf stream; and is, for the reasons already given in the previous chapter, well adapted for the growth of cotton. Doubtless, some of the Kaffirs of Natal, seeing the great care devoted to the production of this staple of our manufactures in that thriving and industrious little colony, will communicate the intelligence to their countrymen, and eventually it may be brought to the notice of their chiefs. If Panda, the great chief of the Zulus, was once convinced of the benefits which would arise to his people by the cultivation of this plant, we should hear no more of bloody wars and wholesale massacres in his dominions; for he would soon learn that the increase of his people would be an increase of his own wealth and power.

It would be well to try the experiment by

presenting Panda with a certain number of pounds of cotton-seed, holding out some great inducement for him to return, at the proper season, a proportionate amount of seed-cotton, which might be easily ginned in the colony. A trade of this sort, once established, would tend greatly to the civilization of the whole Zulu Kaffir race, by which they would, under their own chiefs, be turned to agricultural occupations, affording eventually to Natal a large and immediate supply of labour for the soil, which is all that Natal requires to become the great nucleus of civilization in South Eastern Africa.

On Friday, the 10th of July, 1857, the "Hermes" steamed into Delagoa Bay, known in the history of Eastern Africa as one of the most unhealthy parts of that coast. As we propose investigating the causes of this reported unhealthiness, it will be necessary to describe the bay, and then to examine whether the locality or the visitors are to be most blamed for the great fatality which has taken place amongst those who have visited it.

The Bay of Delagoa, formerly called Formosa

Bay, from the security of the anchorage and beauty of the scenery, is a deep inlet of the Indian Ocean, formed by the stream, known in the Atlantic as the Gulf Stream, constantly setting to the southward along the east coast of Africa.

The abrading influence of this current has been arrested in the south part of the bay by the firmer and loftier formation of the country, assisted by the continual deposits brought down to their mouths by the Mapoota and English rivers, which flow into the south side of the bay.

The current having been deflected thus from the mainland, in its easterly set, while returning to the ocean, has formed for itself a channel, by separating a lofty headland from the main and forming of it the island now called Iniack.

The bay thus forms an arc, on the chord of which may be found large shoals, and even islands, formed by the action of this great stream, and the natural deposits of two large rivers, which discharge themselves into the upper or north-western portion of the bay, called respectively the Magaia or Esperito Santo, and the King George's or Manakusi.

The anchorage of the bay lies mainly in the mouth of the English River, which there runs due east and west, and it may, therefore, be imagined how secure is this anchorage, land-locked from all winds, and protected from the sea by a number of islands and shoals placed as natural breakwaters.

Nature could not well have formed a bay more admirably adapted for the purpose of holding communication with the interior of the adjoining country.

To seaward, open on all sides to this bay and the Indian Ocean, forming the southerm arm of Delagoa Bay, is Iniack Island, which is 240 feet in height, and shows no indication of a sickly climate; but, on the contrary, has been always used by the natives of the adjoining low country of Tembe (which forms the south side of the bay) as a sanitarium.

Inland, on the north bank of the English River, is a lofty cliff, called Point Rubin, gradually declining into the interior to the banks of the adjoining rivers. This would be almost as healthy a locality as the former, although, of course, it would not have the advantage of the pure and bracing breezes from the Indian Ocean.

The remainder of the bay may be pronounced a dead flat, extending into the interior for many miles; and, in viewing the bay, the simplest idea of self-preservation, which, we are told, is the first law of nature, would at once suggest that in such a locality there were only the two above named places for the erection of a town. To make this matter plainer, we have only further to observe that the lowness of the surrounding extent of country, the humid atmosphere arising from the surface of a bay wherein the great Gulf Stream constantly circulates, and the malaria which must naturally arise from the mouths of four considerable rivers discharging the drainage of large tracts of country, and, before disemboguing themselves, traversing flat districts where their streams are sluggish and overcharged with masses of decayed and decaying substances, must naturally lead to a state of the atmosphere, in the bay tending to generate, with the heat of the climate, those virulent forms of fever known under the name of marsh and putrid.

With the above description of this lovely bay, it will only be necessary to state that the most unhealthy spot has been chosen for the erection of a town; which will at once explain the reason of the unhealthiness of the Portuguese settlement of Lourenço Marques.

This town derives its name from a Portuguese, who first established the ivory trade, at this place, with the natives of the country. It is situated on the north bank of the English River, almost at the foot of the high red cliff which forms the south and eastern face of Point Rubin; consequently, all the heat and glare from this cliff is reflected on the unhappily-situated settlement from sunrise until three o'clock in the afternoon. Between the town and the river there is a high sand-bank, which effectually cuts off the sea-breeze. In the rear of the town there is a swamp, or marsh, which is at once the destruction and salvation of the settlement, for, while its pestiferous breath pollutes the atmosphere, and causes all in its neighbourhood to breathe the air of death, its slimy nature, depth, and treacherous bottom prevent the onslaught of the natives, with which the Portuguese are constantly threatened; for which reason the only two field-pieces which the garrison possesses are pointed towards this, their best friend and worst foe.

The town consists of a miserable square of squalid-looking houses, surrounded by huts containing the natives whom the occupants of the ruinous-looking habitations have enslaved. This miserable place is protected by a structure, to which is applied the name of a fort, having a large flag-staff, displaying the flag of Portugal, and a few honey-combed guns, which cannot be fired.

The town is filthy in every sense; even the Governor's quarters being so surrounded with filth and dirt of all sorts, that none but Portuguese and Natives, acclimatized by long usage to the pestilential atmosphere of the place, can approach it without being attacked with fits of vomiting. It is impossible for any one to see the town of Lourenço Marques without being struck with the idea how it is possible for human beings to live there.

I suppose, on the Portuguese first settling in Delagoa Bay, they erected a temporary location on the bank of the river, opposite to where their vessels were at anchor; intending at an early date to remove to the adjoining highland, but that those who were left behind, on their vessels sailing to form the new settlements along the coast, were overtaken by the effects of the malaria of the position which they had first chosen, and that many of them must have fallen victims to this want of foresight in the Commander of the expedition; while the survivors found themselves too enfeebled to undertake the formation of another town in a more healthy locality; and getting gradually acclimatized to the atmosphere of the place, they decided upon remaining where they were.

After the above description of Lourenço Marques, the reader will not be surprised at the unhealthiness of the place, and will seek for its cause, not in the climate of this portion of Africa, but in the locality chosen for this Portuguese settlement. There is a slimy mud bank between Waterloo and Southwark Bridges on the Thames; the occupant of a hut built on that mud bank would, in the height of our summer, be nearly as liable to marsh or putrid fever as the inhabitants of Lourenço Marques.

When the Dutch made their appearance on the East Coast of Africa, they built a Fort on English River, opposite to Lourenço Marques; having only one object in view, namely, the wresting of the valuable commerce, then established, from the Portuguese. To place themselves in communication with the natives, and cut them off from Lourenço Marques, their settlement was opposite to that of the Portuguese, and therefore, was like wise unhealthy. The first Dutch Factory was destroyed by the Natives, who were instigated to this by the Portuguese, at a time when the Dutch were disappointed of reinforcements, and demoralized and enfeebled by the pestilential atmosphere of the malaria district, which circumstances somewhat compelled them to choose, in order that they might break up the monopoly of the ivory trade enjoyed by the Portuguese.

The second Factory of the Dutch was built in the same place as the former one; and this they abandoned on the appearance of the English in these waters.

On the Dutch again becoming masters of the Cape of Good Hope, they found that they could not compete with the English, whose superior manufactures, brought by the Banyans from Bombay to Lourenço Marques, had established a trade with which they could not interfere. That trade has been carried on ever since, but has now dwindled down into utter insignificance, in consequence of the difficulties thrown in the way by the Portuguese officials abandoned to the Slave trade. They obtain sufficient American goods for the ivory trade with the Natives; whilst, by excluding the English, they are enabled to carry on the Slave Trade in complicity with the neighbouring chief who may be paramount at the time; and who, being the victor, has more prisoners to supply the odious traffic by which alone the Portuguese Official may hope to make the means of retiring to his own country.

The Portuguese claims to territory on the East Coast of Africa begin at Lourenço Marques, which is the most southern point on the coast where the Portuguese flag is permitted to fly.

Formerly, the authorities of Lourenço Marques

claimed the whole of Delagoa Bay; but the southern portion of the bay, comprehending Tembe and its dependency, Iniack Island, having been ceded to Captain W. F. Owen, R.N., by King Keppel, in 1823, we have been in possession of a tract of country which affords us access to the Zulu country by way of the British river Mapoota, while the English River gives us access into the interior, even, it is believed (for this country is very little known), to the Transvaal Republic.

The Boer States of the Orange Free State and Transvaal Republic have no port, and consequently no outlet for their commerce. Their products have, therefore, to find their way to the ocean by the harbours of the Cape Colony, or that of Port Natal. To avoid the transit dues of import and export, they have turned their attention to Port St. Lucia, as already stated; but this not altogether suiting their purpose, and being on a line of coast in close proximity to Natal, where they may expect to be checkmated by Great Britain extending her authority to Cape Colatto, they have turned their thoughts more directly to

Delagoa Bay; which, from its receiving four large navigable rivers, communicating with the interior and their own States, offers every facility for extending their commerce to the richest portion of Africa. These Boers are very prolific, many of the women bearing upwards of twenty children. I am personally acquainted with three such mothers; and, after a careful calculation, I am inclined to believe that the average of the Boer families is sixteen; and, I may almost say, never less than twelve. It may well be imagined that a people who increase so rapidly, and with whom the south part of Africa is known to agree remarkably, require only an outport to become a mighty nation.

While residing at the Cape of Good Hope, I was informed that the Boers contemplated the purchase of Delagoa Bay; and I am now in a position to state that I know, from undoubted authority, that this arrangement was far advanced.

In the execution of what I conceived my duty to my country, I brought this matter under the notice of Her Majesty's late Government, recalling the cession of Tembe and Iniack Island, and pointing out the advantages of establishing a Factory for the purposes of trade, and also a Lighthouse for steam-postal communication on the last named place, which, from the salubrity of its climate and central position, would soon become an emporium for trade. And I am glad to think that I have been thus far successful in upholding the rights of my country and frustrating the Portuguese intentions of selling, and those of the Boers of buying, British Territory.

The Tembe country abounds in Orchella weeds, which were first discovered by a British subject, not more than three years ago.

It may be recollected that, when at Natal, I stated that Mr. G. W. Duncan handed me a letter relative to slaving transactions going on at Delagoa Bay. During the visit of Mr. Duncan to this place, he discovered that the Orchella weed was to be had in enormous quantities on the South, or British, side of the bay. He persuaded the natives to collect some for him, so as to take it down to Natal as a specimen. On his return to Delagoa Bay, wishing to obtain a cargo of this valuable weed from the Zulus living on the British side of the bay, he commenced operations for that purpose; but the Portuguese Governor, Muchado, of the small settlement of Lourenço Marques, built on the opposite side of English River, informed him that such traffic with the natives was forbidden. In the meanwhile, during his stay at Lourenço Marques, a large vessel was filled up with Orchella weeds and ivory, obtained from the Zulus of Tembe. This vessel had been sent for to Mozambique, by Governor Muchado, when informed of the discovery made by the enterprising Englishman from Natal.

Mr. Duncan had the mortification to see his discovery not only seized upon by the Portuguese, but, at the same time that Governor Muchado forbade him to trade with Tembe, he saw a vessel under the Portuguese flag obtaining the weed which he had discovered in British territory. Truth is stranger than fiction. What Mr. Duncan did at Delagoa Bay on a small scale, Dr. Livingstone has done on a grand scale in the interior; both endeavouring to make discoveries for the benefit of the natives of Africa, and the commerce of their own much-loved country, and—mark the sequel—both with the same results.

Dr. Livingstone has opened the Luavo mouths of the Zambesi to commerce. These mouths were known to the Portuguese before, but they were always reported to be impassable; the object of this being that, while the Portuguese Officials kept our Cruisers at anchor off the Killimane mouth of the river, the Slavers might come in and go out by the Luavo mouths. As soon as Dr. Livingstone had pointed out that these mouths were navigable, and proved it by entering the river by one of those mouths, the Portuguese Government immediately decided upon establishing Custom-houses on the river. Thus are we prevented from trading with the natives of the country, and from benefiting by the enterprise of our countrymen.

This digression was somewhat necessary, to show how our valuable possession of Tembe has been trifled with by the Portuguese in Delagoa Bay.

The Orchella weed is gathered in bags, and a number of these are placed together under a screw press (with which all vessels in this trade are provided), and formed into bales.

As many of my readers are, doubtless, unacquainted with the properties of this valuable weed, the following brief account of it and its habitat may not be unacceptable :—

Dyer's Orchella Weed.—This is one of the most valuable of the vegetable products of Eastern Africa, and may be found, in greater or less quantity, from the Cape of Good Hope to the Red Sea.

There are several species or varieties of this lichen; and it has been used, from the most ancient times, for the purpose of supplying a colouring matter.

Theophrastus, Dioscorides, and Pliny mention a plant which grew near the ground on the rocks of Crete, and was used for dying purple; the last named of these three ancient writers calls this plant *phycos thalassion;* while Dioscorides says that some persons imagine that the paint used by women was made from this plant; but he adds that it was a root bearing this name.

The *phycos thalassion* of the ancients has been usually assumed to be the *Rocilla tinctoria;* and Bory de St. Vincent even thinks that the ancients made their celebrated purple dye, brought from the isles of Elishah, with the *R. tinctoria*, which he therefore calls *R. purpura antiquorum.*

In the fourteenth century, a nobleman, named Ferro, or Fredrigo, of German extraction, while travelling in the Levant, discovered that the colour might be extracted from this plant by the action of urine: in the Levant, this plant was called *respio* or *respo*, and in Spain, *orciglia.* Proceeding to Florence, where his family were settled, he made known his discovery, and it was applied to the dyeing of wool. His family was ennobled for this discovery, under the name of Oricellarii, altered to Rucellai, and became greatly enriched in consequence of the monopoly of the importation of this weed, which they had for some generations. From the name Rucellai, the generic term Rocella is supposed to be derived.

All species and varieties of Rocella found in commerce bear the general appellation of Orchella weed; but they are distinguished by the name of the country from which they are exported.

The commercial kinds of Orchella weed may be conveniently arranged in two divisions.

1st. Orchella weeds having a cylindrical tapering thallus—*Rocella tinctoria.*

Found in the Canary Islands; Western Islands; Cape de Verde Islands; some parts of the coast of Barbary; South America, and the Cape of Good Hope.

2nd. Orchella weeds having a flat (plane) or compressed thallus. These consist of *R. fuciformis*, and perhaps *R. Montagnei.*

Found in Angola (Portuguese Province on the West Coast of Africa); Madagascar; the Portuguese Province of Mozambique, from Cape Delgado to Delagoa Bay, on the East Coast of Africa; South America; and Pondicherry in India.

There is certainly a third description in commerce, known as mixed Orchella weeds, and consisting of varieties of the foregoing, mixed irregularly.

The second division of these Orchella weeds, *R. fuciformis*, is the more valuable, and is known in commerce, in its various forms, under the denomination of the country, as already stated, from which it is imported.

Angola Orchella weed; *R. fuciformis. Thallus*

very flat, seldom exceeding an inch and a-half, or two inches, in length; in breadth (except at the fork or division) rarely more than one-sixth of an inch; colour greenish, or yellowish grey. As a dye stuff, it is the most valuable of all the Orchella weeds.

The above is Dr. Pereira's description of the Angola Orchella weed, and the Mozambique Orchella weed is exactly the same; the Madagascar being smaller, but in other respects similar to the Angola and Mozambique.

Although the Portuguese have had possessions of immense territorial extent, both on the West and East Coasts of Africa, for more than three centuries, in regions where this weed of the most superior quality abounds, it is only within the last twenty or thirty years that they have brought it into the European market; and, from what I could learn at Mozambique, it is only since the Slave Trade was partially checked in that Province, that the Mozambique people began to export this valuable commodity, viz., subsequent to 1850. It abounds in such quantities along the whole of this coast, that literally fleets may be loaded with it.

As this work is written for practical purposes, I offer no apology for inserting what may hereafter be useful in developing the Resources of Eastern Africa.

Mode of extracting the colorific principles for transport. Dr. Stenhouse suggests the following method:—

Cut the lichens into small pieces, macerate them, in wooden vats, with milk of lime, and saturate the solution either with hydrochloric or acetic acid. The gelatinous precipitate is then to be collected on cloths, and dried by a gentle heat. In this way almost the whole colorific matter can be easily extracted, and the dried extract transported, at a small expense, from the most distant inland localities, such as the Andes or Himalayas. Lime along the whole East Coast of Africa may be made from shells and coral.

The Angola, Mozambique, and Madagascar Orchella weeds, being all of the same variety, *R. fuciformis*, are found growing on both trees and rocks; while in other places they are found only on trees, or on rocks.

The country surrounding the magnificent Bay of Delagoa abounds in cattle. In the waters of the bay the sperm whale is to be found; and here American whalers generally call, not only for the purpose of fishing the whale, but also of obtaining some of the far famed ivory which finds an outlet from the interior by means of this bay. The rivers abound with hypopotami; and the natives kill them, either by means of pits, which they dig on the banks of the rivers, or by means of large stakes of wood attached to the branches of trees. These stakes are sometimes pointed with the barb of a large iron arrow, or the head of an assigay; and to make them heavy, so as to pene trate the skin of the hypopotamus, the stakes are loaded with stones, which are attached to them. One of the numerous creeping or climbing plants, found in abundance, are used to suspend the stake thus prepared, while the end of the cord or plant is led across the path where the hypopotamus is expected to pass. The natives are aware that the animal does not lift his feet off the ground, and therefore avail themselves of this peculiarity to make him his own executioner.

The foot of the beast coming in contact with the cord or creeper, laid across his path, disconnects the loaded stake with its poisoned barb; it enters the back of the hypopotamus, and his fate is sealed.

On other occasions, the Natives in their canoes approach the hypopotamus, and lance their poisoned arrows and assigays at the monster, while sporting in the river. The river horses, feeling themselves wounded, dive to the deepest holes in the river; but they are not lost to the eye of the vigilant savage. To the arrow or lance, firmly imbedded in the body of the monster, a long line is attached, which has on the end of it an inflated bladder, this buoys the spot where the hypopotamus is breathing his last; and in twenty-four hours, or less, according to the potency of the poison used, and the vulnerability of the place struck, the huge carcase floats; when the Natives tow it to the shore, and enjoy the rich repast which their industry and ingenuity has provided for them. The teeth of these monsters are very good ivory. I endeavoured to obtain both here, and also at Killimane, the skeleton of one, pointing out to the Portuguese that the ants would soon clean the bones, if they would pack them up, and send them to me at Mozambique. I even offered a handsome amount for a fœtus, which might often be obtained from the females which they kill, intending to forward it to my friend, Professor Owen. But the truth is, the Portuguese all laughed at the idea of troubling themselves with any specimens in natural history beneath the dignity of man. Of man in all his varieties, male and female, and of all ages, from lisping infancy to decrepid age, I could have had any number at my own price; frequently for two dollars per specimen, and sometimes even for half that price.

Rice, Indian corn, or mealies, milho (small grain for the use of the slaves), simsim seed, yams, cassava, &c., and nearly all the European vegetables, will grow well and abundantly, if sown in a shady place, under lofty trees, and well watered. Potatoes, when a foot above the ground, ought to have the plant broken, not off, but so that it will lie on the ground; this will promote the growth of the bulb; otherwise the plant would grow to a great height at the expense of the root. English and Mapoota Rivers are both said to take their rise in the Transvaal Republic, the following brief notice of which may not be unacceptable to the reader anxious to obtain an insight into the riches of a hitherto unknown country.

The Transvaal Republic is divided into six principal divisions, viz. :—

1. Potchefstroom, or Mooi River Drop, which is the capital of the Transvaal Republic, said to be a village of some extent, but as yet thinly built upon. It is watered by the Mooi River, a narrow and rapid stream, said to take its rise about fifteen miles above the town, and to flow into the Vaal River, about twenty miles after passing the town. This district is not reported as being very inviting to emigrants.

2. Pretoria Philadelphica, situated on the south side of the Magaliesberg, or Eushan Mountains, contains only seven houses, and yet is said to have as numerous a population as any other district in the Republic. It is spoken of as the most salubrious, picturesque, and productive of the Transvaal districts.

3. Rustenburg is situated on the north of the Magaliesberg, and lies about seventy miles west by north from Pretoria Philadelphica. This is a most fruitful district, but like most of those situated to the northward of the Magaliesberg Mountains, it is excessively hot in the summer season; very trying to adults, and although not fatal to children, yet during the hot season there is much sickness among them.

4. Zoutpansberg is the northern boundary of the Transvaal country. The southern side of the mountain has a climate similar to that of Rustenberg, but to the northward of the mountain the climate is said to be bad. Persons crossing it, in the summer months, have been frequently attacked with fever of a very pernicious character; and, it is said, have brought yellow fever into the small village of Schoemansdel, which lies under the mountain. In consequence of this a law has been passed that no one shall cross the mountain between the months of October and May. This district seems principally inhabited by ivory hunters, who have not as yet been compelled to turn their attention to the soil.

5. Waterberg is situated between Pretoria and Zoutpansberg, at a distance of about seventy miles from the former, in a northerly direction. It is said to be very beautiful, more especially the more mountainous portions of it. The climate is similar to that of Rustenberg.

In this district, horse sickness, which is at times so destructive at the Cape and Natal, appears to be very prevalent. To the Boers, who may be said to be always in the saddle, this is very distressing, and a great drawback to the other advantages of the district. Even horses which have had the sickness at Natal, and are therefore considered proof against it, and are termed "salted horses," here suffer as if they had not been seasoned. But those which have been "salted" in the neighbouring Orange Free State are said to be proof against the horse sickness in this district.

A horse, which at Natal might be purchased for from ten to twelve pounds sterling, will consequently bring from sixty to eighty pounds if properly salted.

6. Zuiker Bosch Rand is a hilly district, lying

about twenty miles north of the Vaal River. It is said to be the highest land in the Transvaal country, and therefore one will not be surprised to hear that it is the most healthy. Sheep do here remarkably well, and some quantity of wool is produced; while horses are as healthy on the highest portions of the district as at Natal.

The Transvaal country has been long celebrated for abundance of game; but here, as in the other portions of South Africa, it is rapidly disappearing, and, before the end of this century, will probably be one of those things which have been.

In the more southerly or cooler districts, that is to say, in Potchefstroom, or Mooi River Drop, and Zuiker Bosch Rand, the white-tailed gnu, blesbok, sprigbok, hartebeest, are still numerous; whilst toward the source of the Vaal River elands and the common quagga are met with.

North of the Magaliesberg the roybok or pallah, the brindled gnu, springboks, zebras, giraffes, rynosters, hartebeest, bastard hartebeest, khooder, waterbuck, gemsbuck, the harris, or zwart wit-pens buck, the striped eland, discovered by Livingstone on the Shesheke, the buffalo and the elephant, are still to be found within the Transvaal territory.

The government, foreseeing the rapid disappearance of the game, has passed a law forbidding any one to waste the flesh of any wild animal, under a penalty ranging from three to fifteen pounds for each offence, according to the size of the animal. It is hoped that this will check the indiscriminate slaughter carried on to obtain the skins of the animals.

Immediately to the north of the Transvaal country, the elephant is found in plenty. During the summer months, Tetse fly and yellow fever take up their abode in the northern side of the Zoutpansberg; but about the middle of May, when the fever has disappeared, the hunters of the Transvaal set out on foot, accompanied by Kaffirs to carry their guns, ammunition, and provisions, and to bring in the ivory and rhinoceros' horns.

Boers, from the age of fourteen to that of even seventy, may be seen engaged in the hunt; and it is said that one William Fitzgerald, an Englishman, carries off the palm as being the most fearless hunter in the Transvaal country. It is stated that last year he remained in the veldt without cover for nearly three months, during which time he was accompanied by two half-castes in his employ. These three are said to have killed, during that period, seventy elephants, the tusks of which weighed upwards of 3,000 lbs. This man has, during twelve years as a hunter, encountered as marvellous adventures as Gordon Cumming, which some day he may communicate to the world.

In the Transvaal, wheat and other cereals thrive well. Tobacco is produced in large quantities. All the fruits of the temperate zone are said to be abundant; while, in the Magaliesberg district, oranges, lemons, grapes, figs, peaches, apples, pears, apricots, with musk and water melons, may be had in any quantity.

A Boer, of the name of Roos, has been growing the sugar-cane to the north of the Magaliesberg, and has succeeded in making sugar.

The country is reported to be almost as well watered as Natal; and that, we know, has a stream about every four miles.

The much-disputed source of the Limpopo is now said to be in the Web Water Rond, a range of hills running parallel to Magaliesberg; Elephant River is stated to run into the Maputa, or English River, both of which discharge themselves on the south side of Delagoa Bay.

Apies River and Pienaars River are reported as running into the Limpopo, near the boundary of the district of Rustenberg, on the confines of the Transvaal; while the Limpopo is thought to be the Manakusi, or King George's River, running into the north part of Delagoa Bay.

The country of the Transvaal is rich in mineral productions. The rocks are primary, with but here and there a superstratum of lime-stone. A German miner, Dr. Dousterswivel (?), has succeeded in persuading the Government that he can make a lead mine pay, and is working it for the benefit of the state. Copper and plumbago are to be found there in great quantity, and also in close proximity to Delagoa Bay. Already the Transvaal republic supplies the Orange Free State, and also Natal, with grain; and, when well governed, its destiny, whether as an independent state, or one of the future federated South African states, under British protection and rule, must be great.

The recent expedition of the British cutter, "Herald," up the Manakusi river, has shown its capabilities for navigation and commercial intercourse with the interior; and, if it should be proved that this is the outlet of the Limpopo, it is not the miserable hybrids at the Portuguese factory of Lourenço Marques who will prevent British traders establishing themselves on some healthy elevation in Delagoa Bay.

The value of the exports of these industrious Boers, in a few years, when they have settled themselves, and turned their attention to the riches of the soil, both on the surface and below it, may be estimated from the fact that, last year, in the short space of three months, the ivory obtained by the Boers, in Zoutpansberg alone, was computed at 60,000 pounds weight Dutch, or nearly thirty tons.

CHAPTER IX.

Appearance of the Coast to the North of Delagoa Bay—Facility of Shipping Slaves—Slavers' Signals—Rivers Lagoa and Inhampura—Cape Corrientes—"Sail, ho!"—The Chase—"Zambesi"—Ex-Governor Leotti—A Slaver Clears from Cardiff—Inhambane—Products—Mineral Wealth.

SOON after anchoring in Delagoa Bay, and while the boat was getting ready to take Captain Gordon and myself on shore, the Captain of an Arab brig, lying at anchor opposite to the town, came on board the "Hermes," accompanied by some other Arabs. These Arabs or Moors recognized Mr. Soares, to whom they appeared to be well-known, and they willingly took charge of some dispatches for the Governor of Lourenço Marques.

The delivery of these dispatches was the only cause of our visiting the bay, besides that of looking in to see if the "Minnetonka," or some other slaver, might not be loading with a cargo of slaves, provided for her by the accommodating Governor Mochado, of whom we shall have to speak further during this truthful narrative.

Finding the "Minnetonka" could neither be seen nor heard of at Delagoa Bay, after a stay of only two hours, we proceeded in search of her to the northward; steaming close in shore up to Cape Corrientes, which we had heard at Natal was the point on the coast which she was to make.

Steaming along this coast, we remarked that all the trees, or rather bushes (for they were not higher), close along the sandy beach, had an inclination towards the south-west, showing the fury with which the hurricanes, coming down the Mozambique Channel, strike this coast from the north-east.

Numbers of the natives came down to the coast, and kept company with the ship by running along the sandy beach. Along nearly the whole of this coast, it is quite apparent that, if the native chiefs are willing, slavers can easily ship their cargoes; for there are few places where a vessel could not anchor, send the planks of her slave-deck on shore, and with these construct a raft, and warp it, laden with negroes, from the shore to the ship.

In all these parts the slave-dealers must have agents to procure the natives they require to keep up a regular supply for the traffic. On the high ridge of land running parallel to the beach, and at from three to ten miles inland, might be observed fires lighted up to herald our approach. At times we could almost imagine that we were overtaking these, but when we came nearly abreast of the latest beacon, and were keeping a bright look out for our anticipated prize, another and yet another fire on the hills would tell how we were baffled, and how well the slave-dealers were served. Of course this could only have been done with the connivance of the native chiefs; and while it shows how fearfully the Portuguese have abused their position on this coast, it convinces one that they are not without influence among the natives, and that if they can use it for such a purpose, they might be equally successful in employing it in ameliorating the condition of the blacks, whom they now use only as objects of barter with the man-stealer. The natives observed on shore were armed with lances, and bows, and arrows; and viewing them through the telescope, they looked a well-developed, warlike race. The natives between Delagoa Bay and Sofala have always been a subject of great anxiety to the Portuguese ever since their settlement in Eastern Africa.

There are numerous rivers running down to the coast to the southward of Inhambane, and indeed it is said to be one of the best watered portions of this side of the great continent. Some of these rivers are navigable for small craft; but all are more or less difficult of access in consequence of the bars at their entrance, formed by their own deposit at their mouths, being acted upon by the stream already named and the local monsoons.

The rivers Lagoa and Inhampura, the former in latitude S. 25° 21′, and the latter nine miles further to the northward, being in latitude 25° 12′ S., are both said to be navigable for some distance, and give a ready access to a country abounding in the richest productions of this coast. But the blight of slavery is on the whole district; and the knowledge of the natives of this part regarding Europeans is that the object of the white man in approaching them is to make slaves of them. For more than three centuries the Portuguese have been located at the neighbouring town of Inhambane, and during the whole of that time the unfortunate child of Africa has been taught to believe this. Three centuries is a long time for a barbarian people to hold such a belief. How much longer shall this continue?

Coming abreast of Cape Corrientes early on the morning of the 11th of July, we could see our approach heralded from hill to hill by the beacon fires which were immediately lighted.

North and south the smoke of these fires was seen as far as the eye could reach, alarming the whole coast.

Off Cape Corrientes nothing like a vessel could

be seen, but, while searching the bight of land between Cape Wilberforce and Barrow Hill, a sail was reported from the mast-head.

"Where away?"

"Two points on the starboard bow, sir."

"Port!—port the helm!"

"Port it is, sir!"

"The sail bears right ahead now, sir."

"Very well. Steady as she goes, quarter-master!"

"Steady it is, sir!"

"Engine-room, there!"

"Sir."

"Draw forward the fires under the spare boiler, and set on full speed!"

"Ay, ay, sir!"

"How is her head, master?"

"East-north-east, sir!"

"Steer very steady."

"Ay, ay, sir."

Such were the rapid questions and answers exchanged immediately after the cry of "Sail, ho!" from the mast-head man.

The shovelling of coal, and banging of furnace

doors, might be distinctly heard from the engine-room, on the quarter-deck.

The whole ship was in a commotion. Cape Corrientes in sight, and a strange sail reported to seaward.

The ward-room officers had just sat down to dinner, when the cry of "Sail, ho!" made them all, with the exception of the doctor, who was too fond of creature comforts, rush upon deck. The master repaired to the steering-wheel, to superintend the steerage of the vessel.

The senior lieutenant walked quietly forward to the forecastle, and cast his scrutinizing eyes on the "long gun," and then on the stranger. The second lieutenant, unbidden, bent his way up the fore-rigging, his telescope slung over his shoulder, and perched himself on the fore-topmast cross-trees. Over his head, leaning on the fore-top-gallant-yard, he perceived Mr. Bliss, telescope in hand, examining the stranger.

Mr. Midshipman Bliss, who had kept the fore-noon watch, having dined, and worked out the position of the ship, for want of some more interesting occupation, had betaken himself to sleep, and was having a very comfortable "caulk" when the cry of "Sail, ho!" had disturbed him in a pleasant dream of home and promotion.

With a sort of instinct he rushed immediately to the mast-head, and although only half awake, he was able to make out that the stranger was long, low, and rakish.

To the lieutenant's hurried inquiry, "What do you make of her?" Mr. Bliss replied, "Well, sir, I do not know whether it is the haze or the sleep in my eyes, but she appears to loom very large."

After overhauling her with his glass, the lieutenant remarked that she was "long, low, and rakish, but did not look much of a craft."

Meanwhile, the steam was getting up in all the boilers, and the "Hermes" was closing on the chase.

The gunner was moving mysteriously about the deck with priming wires, vent bits, and detonating matches, evidently bent on mischief.

The watch below had all gone on deck, and the ship's deck was crowded with anxious faces directed towards the chase.

The senior lieutenant, who was no stranger in these waters, having served as a midshipman in the ship of a well-known commodore on this station, spoken of to this day as "Old Ben Wyvell," suddenly turned round, and facing the "bridge" on which the captain was looking out, exclaimed, "She's about, sir — the chase has tacked."

At the same moment the middy's voice from the mast-head was heard :—

"The chase is in stays, sir!" — indicating that she was going about on the other tack.

Soon after, the stranger was observed to bear up, and crowding all sail, to steer for the land.

The excitement throughout the ship was now at its greatest pitch.

Soon after it was reported that negroes in great numbers were observed upon her deck.

Meanwhile, the chase was kept upon the same bearing, and, as the two vessels neared each other, for we gained on the chase, they approached closer and closer to the land.

We were now off the harbour of Inhambane; and it was evidently the intention of the stranger either to beach herself, or to run into Inhambane harbour, under the protection of the fort, when we could not board her without the sanction of the Portuguese authorities.

The vessel was urged to the utmost, under the power of steam; but still it was evident that the stranger sailed well, and, under her crowd of canvas, it was feared that she might attain one of the two objects which she had evidently in view.

During the whole of the chase, the "Hermes" displayed the British ensign and pennant, but the stranger showed no colours.

At last, moments became hours, and the stranger stood boldly on to destruction on the reefs, or safety under the Portuguese flag at Inhambane.

"Clear away the 'long gun,' and load with blank!"

In a minute was heard the report, "The gun is ready, sir!"

"Very good—Fire!"

Bang went the fifty-six pounder, and when the smoke cleared away, the stranger was seen holding on the same course.

Meanwhile we had shoaled our water, and the "leads-men" were ordered "into the chains."

Numbers of negroes might now be seen with the naked eye, on the deck of the stranger, which was a large brigantine, evidently armed to fight her way, as the muzzles of one or two guns were observed protruding from her side.

"Forecastle, there!"

"Sir?"

"Load again—with shot!"

"Ay, ay, sir."

"All ready, sir."

"Who fires the gun?"

"Mr. Carr, sir, the gunner."

"Tell him to drop a shot under the stern of the chase; but to be careful not to strike her!"

"Now, Mr. Carr, you hear the order—'Drop a shot under her stern, but do not strike her.'"

"Very good, sir!" "Muzzle to the right," "Muzzle to the left"—"Well"—"Elevate"—"Lower"—"Well"—"Fire!"

Bang went the gun, and the shot was seen to strike the water close to the taffrail; the water splashing over the quarter-deck of the chase. This appeared somewhat to alarm those on board. A flag was hoisted abaft, but being rolled up, it was impossible to make out what colours she displayed.

Still the stranger held on her course, every moment, apparently, hurrying her and all on board to destruction.

"With shot, load!"

"All ready, sir!"

"Fire across her bows, but be careful you do not strike her!"

"Ay, ay, sir."

In less than a minute, a fifty-six pound shot dropped under the bow of the stranger, covering her bowsprit with a cloud of foam. This appeared to bring her commander to his senses, for the anchor was immediately let go, and amidst the din of the chain-cable rattling out of the hawse-hole, and the most fearful yelling and shouting—interspersed with which might be heard the stentorian lungs of a ruffian uttering the most awful oaths, in the vilest of Portuguese—she came head to wind.

As for ourselves, the leads-men's cry of a "half-three" told us that we were just on the reefs. By stopping and reversing the engines quickly, the "Hermes" was saved; but a few yards further, and we would have been on the coral reefs outside of Inhambane harbour.

As soon as the safety of H.M.S. "Hermes" would allow, a boat, with a lieutenant in command, was sent to board the stranger, which, now that she was at anchor, was observed to display the Portuguese ensign and pennant.

On the return of the boat, we learned that the stranger's name was the "Zambesi;" that her rig was that of a patacheo or brigantine; that she was a vessel of war, belonging to His Most Faithful Majesty Don Pedro the Fifth, King of "Portugal and Algarves;" and that she had on board of her a Moor, who stated that he was in temporary command of her, while embarked with him was no less a personage than His Excellency the Ex-Governor of Inhambane. The Moor appeared to be entirely under the orders of the Ex-Governor of Inhambane, who wore the uniform of a Portuguese naval officer; and, when asked why he had not hove-to and communicated with a steamer, which, from her English ensign and appearance, must have been known at once for one of Her Britannic Majesty's cruisers, he referred the lieutenant to the Ex-Governor of Inhambane. This officer, who was very much confused, could, or would not, give any explanation of his personating a slaver, by which we had lost valuable time, and perhaps a prize, and Her Majesty's ship had been greatly jeopardized.

We subsequently learned that the Ex-Governor of Inhambane was Senhor Leotti, a Capitain de Corvette in the Portuguese Navy, and that he had left Inhambane that morning, after an ineffectual attempt to usurp the government from his successor, Major Olliveira.

It will be further shown, during the course of this personal narrative, that this Captain Leotti, a commander in the Portuguese navy, had in the "Zambesi" schooner, belonging to the Royal Navy of Portugal, communicated with the "Minnetonka" slaver that we were in search of on the first of July, the very day, it will be recollected, that we anchored off Port Natal, in the "Hermes."

It will be proved by the clearest evidence,

taken on oath, in documents laid before the British Parliament, that this slaver, the "Minnetonka," lay at anchor off Barrow Hill, outside of Inhambane harbour, flying American colours; that while so lying at anchor off Inhambane, where she had anchored for a cargo of slaves, the Portuguese schooner "Zambesi," with the ensign and royal pennant of Portugal flying, approached the slaver "Minnetonka," and instead of capturing her, as she was bound to do by treaties with Great Britain (for the slaver was within gun-shot distance of the beach), made arrangements for supplying the slaver "Minnetonka" with slaves.

And it will be shown that when the British consul asked the Governor-general of Mozambique for a copy of the sentence of the court which had acquitted the Ex-Governor Leotti, and the Moor commanding the "Zambesi," of the charge made against them, the consul's house was mobbed by natives sent by the slave-dealers to endeavour to intimidate him; and during the stoning, which was indulged in by the natives against his house, his wife was wounded. All these things will be seen; and the reader is only now advised to bear in mind what has already been seen of the "Zambesi," and those on board of her.

The harbour of Inhambane forms the mouth of a large river which has hitherto been unexplored, and is by some believed to be the Limpopo.

Sufficient is, however, known to justify one in stating that it communicates with the interior for a great extent, and that the country through which it has its course is rich in all the products of Eastern Africa.

Timber, of a large and superior quality, may be had in considerable quantities, while the harbour offers every facility for loading vessels with it. But, at the same time, it is proper to state that a cargo of timber has not been sent from this harbour within the memory of man; the only trade carried on being that in human beings.

Shortly before we arrived off the port, a large vessel had gone into the harbour, partly laden with coals. While going in, it appears she struck on the reef, and suffered considerable damage.

I was afterwards favoured with the history of this vessel by the Governor-general of the province of Mozambique. His Excellency's statement was as follows:—

That a large three-masted vessel, under Spanish or English colours—he was not certain which—had loaded with a cargo of coals at Cardiff, in South Wales, in 1856, and had cleared for the Philippine Islands. As soon as the master of the vessel found himself to the eastward of the Cape of Good Hope, he commenced throwing the coals overboard, and arrived at Inhambane with only sufficient coals to serve as ballast. On his arrival in the harbour, he endeavoured to repair the damage sustained while entering it, and for this purpose he placed the vessel on the beach. While undergoing the necessary repairs, she was irreparably injured in consequence of not having been shored up properly, and the captain abandoned her. He had gone into Inhambane for the purpose of receiving a cargo of slaves, arrangements for which, it appears, had previously been made by parties in England.

I endeavoured to obtain the name of this vessel, in order to trace those connected with her; but I was told that the name had been carefully obliterated from her stern, and also from her main hatchway, where some said they had seen it. The different names given to me as belonging to the vessel were certainly English, but I was not able to satisfy myself fully as to the truth of her being an English vessel. The Governor-general told me that the captain said that he had destroyed all the papers before visiting Mozambique, where he repaired after the wreck of his vessel. The captain spoke English and Spanish fluently.

From the intimate acquaintance which some merchants in England have with notorious slave-dealers at Mozambique, I am inclined to credit statements which have been made relative to British capital being engaged in this horrid traffic in our fellow-beings.

It will be seen in subsequent pages that I have brought under the notice of the government that an English vessel was employed to seize natives in the Pacific, and convey them to the French island of Reunion, where they were sold at 40*l.* sterling per head.

The town of Inhambane consists of a few ill-built houses, thatched with the leaves of the cocoa-nut tree, built along the margin of the harbour, or interspersed among the cocoa-nut and mango trees growing along the beach. Of these structures there are about one hundred and fifty, containing in all about seven hundred persons, including Portuguese, Canareens, Moors, and free blacks.

The governor is appointed by the King of Portugal or the Governor-general of Mozambique, for the time being, and is supposed to have a company of soldiers, numbering sixty, but he has seldom half that number for his protection. The soldiers are picked out of those who misbehave themselves at Mozambique; and as the garrison of that place consists of the refuse of the convict regiments at Goâ, who are sent to Mozambique as a further punishment, it may be imagined what a thorough set of scoundrels the Inhambane company are. They are, from time to time, reinforced by the natives, either degenerate Moors or Caffres, who are called upon to mount guard, while the veterans take care of a building styled a hospital, either as inmates, orderlies, or guards.

The malingerers and the recruits, forming the force called "the garrison," are commanded by a captain, lieutenant, and alfares, or ensign; while the most thorough-going and boldest villain among the convicts is picked out for a non-commissioned officer to awe and outwit his comrades. Some of these Portuguese soldiers have outraged every law, human and divine; on this side of the grave there is no hope for them. Banished from their country to Goâ, they have there, in that sink of iniquity, committed fresh crimes, for which they have been sent, as an additional punishment, to Mozambique. Reckless of all consequences, condemned to carry a musket for the remainder of their lives, on a miserable pittance which, unaided, will not support life, they break out of the fort at night, and continue the course of robbery and crime which they had commenced many years previously in Portugal, until their excesses deprive them of life, or lead to their detection; when they are drafted off to Lourenço Marques, Inhambane, Killimane, or some other of the Portuguese settlements on this coast. When corporal punishment is inflicted, it is very severe, and usually with the intention of depriving the culprit of life. The particulars are too revolting to be communicated.

The church is also represented at Inhambane by a "Vigário," or Curate; who, besides his religious duties, engages in commercial pursuits. The character of this "holy man" is aptly described, by one of his own countrymen, as being "*Mais cobiçoso e avaro que os seculares, e mais engolfado queelles na vileza dos vicios*;"—"More covetous and avaricious than the laymen, and more deeply instructed than them in the vileness of their vices."

Justice is also represented; but not by the blind goddess of communities less advanced than the people of Inhambane. Here, he who bribes highest wins his suit.

In short, all the officers necessary for carrying on a good government are appointed; some without salaries, and others with salaries which are a mockery, and all without even a public place in which they can transact business. Doubtless the imperial government of Portugal has supplied the means for these buildings, and they exist, but only on paper. The funds for erecting them having been embezzled by some Governor-general, and his subordinates, who may now be basking in the sunny rays of the court of Lisbon.

The principal edifice is a church, in a deplorable state of ruin; the roof being thatched with the leaf of the palm, and within and without bearing witness to the neglect of that religious faith which it was built to propagate.

Leaving this melancholy picture of man's degradation, let us proceed into the country, beyond the limit of so-called civilization, and explore the vast field which nature here unfolds to us.

In the district of Inhambane, the valleys, the mountains, and the rivers abound in riches. Copper, gold, and iron are found in abundance; nuts, roots, and even trees, are found producing dyes.

The juice of the India-rubber tree affords amusement for the little black boys of Inhambane, who chew it until it becomes plastic, and then inflating it with their breath, are pleased with the report which the bladder makes on bursting. The same amusement may be witnessed among the children of Europe. This is mentioned to show how plentiful India-rubber is in the neighbourhood of Inhambane.

Oranges and lemons are found in great abundance, while grapes grow here on trees, as on the married or grafted trees in Portugal. With these, wine and vinegar are both made. The banana, plantain, and pine apple are very delicious, and abound everywhere.

All the fruits of Brazil are found here as if indigenous to the climate, and in equal perfection; while the country produces trees, herbs, plants, roots, and nuts, having medicinal qualities (see Appendix).

Cocoa-nut trees, the coffee-tree, bearing a small berry, similar in flavour to Mocha coffee, and the sugar-cane, are found in great perfection; the last named being large, and affording abundance of saccharine matter.

Cotton is growing over the whole country; and indigo is *everywhere*.

The Kaffirs bring in plenty of ivory, hunting the elephants with poisoned bows and arrows, and sometimes digging pits for them.

The sea washes up large quantities of amber, while both descriptions of turtle are found along the coast. The sperm whale may be seen in the season off the harbour; and the sea and rivers abound with varieties of delicious fish.

The natives are a warlike race, and appear to keep the Portuguese in good order, but all their prisoners taken in war are supplied for the slave trade. It is unnecessary to state that many of these wars are occasioned by the demands of that inhuman traffic.

The huts of the natives of Inhambane are built square, instead of round, like those of the Kaffirs, and are sometimes made of mud bricks, but more commonly of wattle-dab, or palm leaves. Their manners and customs are very much like those of the natives met with on the Zambesi, of whom we purpose giving some account.

CHAPTER X.

Kingdom of Mocoranga—Kotba for the Soudan of Cairo—Sultan of Kilwa—Kingdom of Algarves—Remains of Ancient Cities—Inscriptions Not Deciphered—Zimboë Bruce—Sofala, the Ancient Ophir—Productions—The Manica Gold Mines—Surrounding Region Adapted for Europeans—Industry of the Natives—The Priests Rob the Jewels from the Image of the Blessed Virgin.

CAPTAIN GORDON having satisfied himself that the "Zambesi" was a Portuguese schooner of war—for from the number of negroes on board of her, and the confusion of Ex-governor Leotti, there were serious doubts entertained whether or not she were a slaver—we steamed away to the northward, keeping a bright look-out for the "Minnetonka," and other slavers known to be on the coast.

Before proceeding further in a description of this interesting coast-line, perhaps it would be as well to explain that on the first arrival on this coast of the Portuguese discoverers, at the commencement of the sixteenth century, they found existing in the interior a large kingdom called Mocoranga, which reached to the coast, along which it extended from the northern portion of Delagoa Bay to the mouths of the river Zambesi, being bounded on the north by that river.

This kingdom was fast falling into decay, and appears to have been the remains of a much greater one, which was partially destroyed or broken up, at some remote period, by the invasion of a warlike people known as the Lindens.

At the principal places along the coast the Portuguese found Arab settlements established, which appeared to be under the dominion of a Sultan at Kilwa, to whom they all looked up as their common local head, while the Kotba, or prayer on Friday, was offered for the head of the Arab family, who at that time was Kansu-el-Ghauri, Soudan of Cairo, called also the Mamlook Sultan of Egypt.

The Sultan of Kilwa was immensely rich in consequence of the vast quantity of gold which he obtained from his dependency of Sofala, which from time immemorial had been the great gold field of the Hebrews and Phœnicians, and even at that time yielded gold in great abundance.

In the course of a few years the Portuguese made themselves masters of these Arab settlements, and thus the Portuguese kingdom of Algarves was formed.

The enterprising Portuguese of those days, having obtained a footing on the coast, soon pushed into the interior, for the purpose of discovering the gold and silver mines of the country; and the natives, instructed by the Arabs, did all in their power to baffle the enterprising Europeans.

During this struggle, the Portuguese made themselves acquainted with the country, and formed settlements on the Zambesi, such as Seña, Tete, and Zumbo, and indeed others, from some of which they were driven to the coast by the natives.

These discoverers and conquerors learned that the kingdom of Mocoranga was very powerful, and the neighbouring vast territory under the Monomotapa more powerful still.

They heard of people who had formerly inhabited these countries, who were far advanced in civilization. And from the west coast of Africa, at the same time, the Portuguese priests were pushing into the interior, to the centres of kingdoms in a state of semi-civilization, where they were at first very successful in making proselytes to the Christian faith, but from which they were eventually banished in consequence of their endeavouring to get the government of those kingdoms into their own hands.

Besides the information thus obtained of the state of civilization then and formerly in that vast continent, rumours reached them of the remains of cities built of large blocks of well-hewn stone. Some of these cities remain until this day, like those in the desert east of the Haurán, and in the ancient land of Bashan, affording an interesting field for the explorer, and bearing inscriptions which neither European nor Arab has yet been able to decipher, but which may be of equal importance with the Adite inscription engraven on the rock at Hishen Goreb.

Feeling deeply interested in this matter, during my residence at Mozambique I did all in my power to obtain information about the Sofala district, which resulted in the Governor-general of the province publishing an official account of the mines known to the Portuguese in that and the surrounding districts, which have been so much neglected by the Portuguese residing there.

This account gives a long list of gold, silver, copper, and iron mines which have been worked, but are now entirely neglected, as the country is destitute of labour — the Portuguese having drained it to supply the slave-trade of the Brazils, Cuba, and America. Previous to which, that district was, as already stated, greatly depopulated by the invasion of the Lindens. These mines still have attached to them the names of the discoverers, and these names are supposed to be those of the kings who reigned there when the mines were first opened.

In this report it is stated that 500 leagues from Seña there are the remains of large edifices, which indicate that they were once inhabited, but by whom is not known.* This confirms the statement of Barros, in his description of the ruins of the city of Zimboë, who states that there are the remains of a fort built of well cut stones, having a surface of twenty-five palms in length, and a little less in height, in the joining of which there appears to have been no lime used. Over the door or entrance of this fort is an inscription which some Moors, well versed in Arabic, could not decipher, nor were they acquainted with the character of the writing.

Around this edifice there are other erections similar to it, having bastions of stone uncemented by lime, and in the middle of them there are the remains of a tower, at least seventy feet in height. These edifices are called, in the language of the country, Zimboë, which signifies a royal residence.

I was told at Mozambique that the Arabs could not decipher the inscriptions to be found at Zimboë.

Barros thinks that the country of Sofala ought to be that designated, by Ptolemy, Agyzimba.

* Boletim do Governo Geral de Provincio de Mocambique, December 12, 1857.

Zimboë, the name of the remains of the royal residences there, certainly offers some affinity to that of Agyzimba; and there is still the remnant of a once powerful nation, called the Zimbas, to be found on the banks of the Zambesi.

Bruce, in the third volume of his travels, tells us, when speaking of the celebrated Portuguese traveller, Covilham, who was detained in Abyssinia, and communicated thence with the King of Portugal, that "in his journal, Covilham described the several ports in India which he had seen; the temper and disposition of the princes; the situation and riches of the mines of Sofala. He reported that the country was very populous; full of cities, both powerful and rich; and he exhorted the king to pursue, with unremitting vigour, the passage round Africa, which he declared to be attended with very little danger, and that the Cape itself was known in India. He accompanied this description with a chart which he had received from the hands of a Moor in India, where the Cape, and cities all around the coast, were exactly represented."

These statements of Bruce are confirmed by

what the Portuguese have reported of the state of the country when they first settled there: that the princes were pure Moors; that their form of worship was the same as that of the Arabs; and that they lived, more especially in the interior, in considerable state.

Among the learned it has been a subject of considerable dispute where the country of Ophir, abounding in gold, was situated.

After a display of great ingenuity and considerable research, in the endeavour to prove Ophir situated in Arabia, India, and even Peru, I think it will be at length allowed that Sofala, on the east coast of Africa, is indubitably the Ophir of Solomon.

"And King Solomon made a navy of ships in Ezion-geber, which is beside Eloth, on the shore of the Red Sea, in the land of Edom. And Hiram sent in the navy his servants, shipmen that had knowledge of the sea, with the servants. Solomon. And they came to Ophir, and fetched from thence gold, four hundred and twenty talants, and brought it to King Solomon."*

* 1 Kings ix., 26-28.

"And the navy also of Hiram, that brought gold from Ophir, brought in from Ophir great plenty of almug trees, and precious stones. And the King made of the almug trees pillars for the house of the Lord, and for the King's house, harps also and psalteries for singers: there came no such almug trees, nor were seen unto this day."*

"For the King had at sea a navy of Tharshish with the navy of Hiram: once in three years came the navy of Tharshish, bringing gold, and silver, ivory, and apes, and peacocks."†

Writers on this subject have endeavoured to prove that this Ophir, where Solomon obtained such immense quantities of gold, is Ofor, on the eastern side of the Arabian peninsula; and that the immense gold-field alluded to by the sacred writer is the adjoining very small extent of coast, known as the *littus Hammæum ubi auri metalla*, or Gold Coast, mentioned by Pliny; asserting that this was the true term of the famous voyage, undertaken in the reign of Solomon, from Ezion-geber, or Akaba, at the head of the Gulf of Elah.

* 1 Kings x., 11, 12.

† Idem, x., 22.

That the small district referred to may have contained a small quantity of gold (as no doubt it does at present, for it is stated to be highly metalliferous), I am not going to dispute.

But we know that Arabia does not contain elephants, and therefore it could not have produced ivory.

The coast line has the pearl oyster, in common with the whole of the Persian Gulf; but not in such abundance as to have been an article of commerce at that place.

Arabia contains no peacocks, nor the guinea-fowl, which is evidently intended by the Hebrew word in the original text.

It never contained apes at the time referred to; for they were introduced into Arabia by Dthoo'l-Adhàr, "the lord of terror," or "the terrible one," who received that epithet in allusion to the frightful animals he had introduced. He reigned in Yemen, during the invasion of Ælius Gallus, which took place in the year one of the Christian era.

The almug tree, supposed by the best authorities to be sandal wood, is not indigenous to Arabia.

Some have gone as far even as Anam, or Cochin-China, for what they believe is this fragrant wood, called in Arabic *A'llawwa*, and in Sanscrit *Aguru*.

Arabia has never produced precious stones in any quantity.

By the extract from the Book of Kings already given, we are told that the voyage to Ophir and back took three years to accomplish, which, if situated in Arabia, might be performed easily in one-third of that time.

It is evident that this Ophir of Solomon was the *Ultima Thule* of the Jews and Phœnicians in the East (or rather South); and if situated in Arabia, it would be approached by land, and not by sea, the latter being in those days a more difficult mode of travelling than the former; and commercial relations being, even at that date, established by land between the Persian Gulf and the Holy Land.

Now, on the other hand, we are distinctly told that "the navy also of Hiram, that brought gold from Ophir, brought in from Ophir great plenty of almug trees and precious stones," showing that these articles were all found at Ophir, and were not imported into that place.

And it will be seen when we describe the produce of Sofala, which we hold to be the Ophir of Solomon, that from time immemorial it has produced, in great abundance, gold, silver, pearls, precious stones, apes and monkeys, and also guinea-fowls, which is supposed, by some authorities, to be the true meaning of the word in the original text which has been translated in our version "peacock."

With reference to the almug trees, I brought to England specimens of the woods to be found on the "Zambesi." Among these specimens is sandal wood, which grows along the whole coast from Delagoa Bay to Mozambique, and is also to be found in great abundance on the opposite side of the Mozambique Channel, on the north-west end of the island of Madagascar, whence it is exported to China. Besides the common sandal wood, which is yellowish-white, I have a specimen of red sandal wood from the "Zambesi," which is very beautiful, not unlike the handsomest specimens of Bermuda cedar, but still having the scent of the common sandal wood, both in the wood of the tree and also that of the root. This I look upon as the almug tree that Solomon made such great use of in the house of the Lord; a specimen of which may be seen at the rooms of the Royal Geographical Society of London.

Finally, we know how the Arabs constantly called places "after their own names,"—what so natural as to call this rich country after the name of their own land? This they positively did; for they call to this hour the river leading from the ocean to the Manica Gold Mines—which are the great mines of the country—the river Sabia; and the large district adjoining Sofala, lying between the rivers Sabia and Sofala, has been, ever since Europeans appeared on that coast, and is now called Sabia; which all persons versed in Arabian history are aware is synonymous with Saba, Sheba, or Yemen; names alike applied to the south part of Arabia, from which the Arabs would naturally start for Africa.*

The great empire of Monomotapa existing in these parts, on the arrival of the Portuguese in

* See Appendix C.

Eastern Africa, was divided into two kingdoms, viz., Monomotapa, or Bonomotapa Proper, and the empire of Mocoranga, which latter comprehended eight kingdoms, as follows:—Carruro-Medra, Mujao, Mukuku, Turgeno, Gengir-Bomba, Manöemouges, Ruenga, and Bororo. Monomotapa Proper also consisted of eight kingdoms—viz., Chikova, Sacumbé, Iñabasé, Munare, Shiroro, Manica, Chingamira, and Sofala.

All these kingdoms were tributary to the Emperor of Monomotapa, except Sofala, which, nominally, belonged to the Portuguese.

The ancient kingdom of Sofala extended north to the Luavo mouth of the Zambesi; and to the south, as far as the river Sofala, formerly to the river Sabia; and west as far as the kingdom of Manica.

The kingdom of Sofala, like all those comprehending Monomotapa Proper, is rich in mines of gold, silver, copper, and iron; precious stones of every variety have been found in this region, and may be obtained in considerable quantities.

The sugar cane, coffee, and indigo are growing everywhere, while wheat is grown on the uplands. All the products already described as appertaining to Inhambane are to be found here; while, if the surrounding district of Monomotapa is included, it may safely be said that there is nothing grown in the torrid and temperate zones which may not be produced in this extensive territory, reaching from the Indian Ocean to the crest of the Lupata Mountains, which are said to be covered with perpetual snow.

The Manica gold mines are situated in a valley, inclosed in an amphitheatre of hills, having a circuit of about 100 miles. The spots containing gold are known by the barren and naked aspect of the surface soil. The district is called Matouca, and the natives who obtain the gold are the Botongos. Although this country is situated between the equator and the tropic of Capricorn, in the cold season the mountains surrounding the mining district are covered with so great a quantity of snow, that, if the natives are caught there at that season, they perish from the cold; but in the hot season, the sides and summits of these mountains enjoy a serene, bracing, equable temperature, while it is hot in the inclosed valleys.

These mountain heights afford at once a desirable residence for Europeans, and will doubtless be found similar in temperature to the upper terraces of Natal.

The natives dig in any small crevice made by the rains of the preceding winter, and there find the gold in dust. They seldom go deeper than one or two feet at the most from the surface, and on digging five or six feet deep, they reach the rock.

There are other mines still farther from Sofala, being about 400 or 500 miles distant, where the gold is found in solid lumps, or as veins in the rocks and stones.

In the still portions of the rivers, when they are low, the natives frequently dive to obtain the lumps of gold which have been washed down into these holes and gullies in the beds of the rivers. They will also sometimes join together in hundreds, and deflect a stream temporarily from its course, to drain these holes, and obtain the rich deposits which they contain. With such natives, what could the Portuguese not do if they would only exert themselves?—but they tell one that the natives are lazy and stupid brutes. On the other hand, the Moors induce the natives to work and obtain gold for them; and so it is very apparent who are deserving of the degrading epithets applied to them by the degenerate hybrid race of Canareens who lord it over them.

On this side of Africa I believe mercury has never been employed for the purpose of extracting the gold, the more valuable metal being so abundant. The natives do not value it, making their ornaments of copper in preference to gold.

The iron from Sofala has been long celebrated for its malleable qualities, and has been carried to India for many ages by the Arabs, where it has always found a ready market.

In the whole of this territory elephants are found; and it has been estimated, from the enormous quantity of ivory produced, that the natives at one time must have killed from three to four thousand of these animals every year.

Along the whole of this coast, the pearl-oyster is to be found. At Inhambane the natives obtain it along the beach without even going out of their depth; while the Bazarutto Islands, near the mouth of the Sabia river, have been long celebrated for the pearl fishery carried on there. It was from these islands that the pearls which accompanied the gold and ivory and precious stones to the court of King Solomon were doubtless obtained.

The Portuguese flag is kept flying at the Bazarutto Islands, but for what purpose, except to keep others from benefiting by the pearls which they neglect, one cannot imagine. From accounts which I have received, I am led to believe that the pearl-fishery at these islands, properly worked and protected, would rival that of Ceylon.

On both banks of the river Sofala, and from that river northwards to the southern bank of the Zambesi, the country is one mass of mineral wealth; gold, silver, copper, and, toward Tete, even iron and coal being found in abundance.

The town of Sofala, which is built at the mouth of the river of the same name, is divided into two portions, one of which contains the Moors, or labourers of the small settlement, and the other the Governor and his subordinates, together with their slaves, who may, collectively, be well styled the drones, for they live by taxes and duties levied on the more industrious Moorish community.

The houses are not unlike those already described at Inhambane, the exteriors by no means leading one to surmise the high-sounding titles of the occupants. That portion of Sofala which is known as Portuguese Town is dirty in the extreme, while the Moorish Town is but little better.

When the Portuguese first appeared on this coast, Sofala was one of those places of which they obtained possession; and Don Pedro da Nhaya built a remarkably fine fort at this place, which remains to this day, a monument of the bygone glory of the nation, and a reproach to the degeneracy of the present race.

At a short distance to the northward of this fort, is a church dedicated to "Our Lady of the Rozario," the walls of which are built of rough stones, while it is roofed in with palm leaves. A covered porch leads to the entrance, on each side of which there is a chamber, one serving as a sacristy, while the other answers as a lodging for the priests. The holy Fathers have no means of support, and are entirely dependent on the alms of the faithful.

Formerly the church was rich in gold and jewels of great value, which adorned the statue of the blessed Virgin; but the priests who sold their fellow-beings into slavery did not hesitate to rob the temple of their God.

There is a great want of water in the town, which might be easily supplied by a pure stream not more than a mile distant; but as there is a large cistern in the fort, built by Da Nhaya upwards of three hundred and fifty years since, they have recourse to this; and neither dig wells nor build an aqueduct.

Of labouring Moors, groaning slaves, and degenerate everybodies, there are said to be 1225 persons.

The military establishment of Sofala is from thirty to thirty-five soldiers, sent from Mozambique for some misdemeanour while serving in that garrison; to these are added a few Moors and Kaffirs, who are shut out of the fort at night, and do double duty by day.

Sofala is admirably situated for commerce; and nothing but the baneful influence of the slave-trade could have reduced it to its present state: a melancholy contrast to the flourishing Arab settlement which the Portuguese found there in 1505.

CHAPTER XI.

The River Zambesi—Luavo Mouths—Killimane—River Shire — Valley of the Shire Abounding in Elephants—How Salt is Made on the Zambesi — From the Ocean to Kaord Vasa Navigable at all Seasons — Water Rises Sixty Feet in Narrows of Lupata—Access to the Cazembe Territory by the Zambesi—Three Seams of Coal Discovered—Products.

THE river Zambesi is one of the most remarkable of the mighty streams of the African continent, and is destined to work great changes in the future of that vast portion of the globe.

The course of this river was but imperfectly known until the recent publication of the travels of the enterprising missionary, Dr. Livingstone.

Like all the great rivers of Africa, it was supposed to have its source in one of two great lakes communicating with each other; and thus it was stated that the Nile, the Niger, the Congo, and the Zambesi had one common origin.

This idea of the most ancient geographers, strictly speaking, has been found to be erroneous; but the march of discovery shows us that, in a general sense, ancient geographical writers had a very fair conception of the physical formation of the interior of Africa.

The existence of a large hydrographical basin, draining Central Africa, and affording the sources of the main streams discharging themselves into the oceans and seas surrounding that continent, has been clearly indicated by Sir Roderick Murchison; while the task of exploring the paths pointed out by this great geologist has been cheerfully undertaken by our countrymen, Livingstone, Burton, and Speke, whose explorations have won for themselves a world-wide celebrity, and maintained for this country the proud pre-eminence of her sons, even in this region, being the first in the path of discovery.

By the achievements of our countrymen at present, we are aware that there are four large lakes in Central Africa, viz., the Nyanza,

Tanganyika, Nyassi or Maravi, and Nyngesi, doubtless affording the sources of the White Nile, the Zambesi, and its feeders, and perhaps, more remotely, those of the Niger.

The object of the present work being to draw attention to East Africa as a rich field for commercial enterprise, geographical and historical disquisitions are studiously avoided, as they have been deemed unsuitable to the general reader, whose attention to this neglected portion of the globe it is my earnest endeavour to attract. I shall, therefore, at once proceed to view this great river in a practical light, remarking upon the products of the country through which it runs, and the suitableness of this stream as a highway for commercial relations between the Indian Ocean and the interior of Africa.

The mouths of the Zambesi extend from 18° to 19° S. Lat., or a distance of 90 miles along the coast. The most southern of these are called the Luavo Mouths, the two principal of which are known as the East and West Luavo Mouths. The East Luavo Mouth was surveyed by the late Captain Hyde Parker, R.N., in 1850; and we also had an imperfect survey of the West Luavo Mouth; but the channels leading from them to the Zambesi at the Boca do Rio were not explored, and therefore deemed unnavigable; although the Portuguese have known all along that these Luavo Mouths were navigable, and they have been used by the Portuguese authorities engaged in the slave-trade for the ingress and exit of vessels engaged in this traffic, while the British cruisers have been detained at anchor off the Killimane Mouth of the river, and their boats have been kept under specious pretexts of information received relative to an embarkation of slaves being about to take place in the Killimane branch of the river, while vessel after vessel was sailing away from the Luavo Mouth full of slaves.

The present Zambesi expedition, under the command of Dr. Livingstone, has dispelled the mystery which hung over the mouths of this great river, for he entered the East Luavo Mouth in the "Pearl" steamer, in June, 1858, and thence ascended the Zambesi in the exploring steam launch, "Ma Robert."

The town of Killimane (Quillimane) stands on the north bank of the most northern mouth of the river, having the same name as that of the town. From the descriptions already given of Inhambane and Sofala, the intelligent reader may draw for himself a picture of this Portuguese town, or, as we should term it, "dirty village."

After leaving Killimane, on the left hand ascending the river, we arrive at Iñhasuja, which is about two leagues from Killimane. Here a stream runs to the sea. On the same side of the river, we next come to Interro, about three and a-half leagues farther, where there is another stream running to the sea. From this place, about four leagues distant, is Maenboosha; about four leagues more, Mangara, where there is another stream running to the sea; three leagues farther is Chataunga; four leagues onwards Mejerumba; and six leagues farther is Mazaro, at the Boca do Rio. This was believed to be the main mouth of the river, as its name indicates. A long musket shot from Mazaro, on the same side of the river, but looking down the Luavo, is Maruro.

The tide reaches Mangara, which is about twelve or thirteen leagues from Killimane.

It takes three days going from Killimane to Mangara by water, in the native boats or large Portuguese launches, while by land one may reach the same place in one day.

Boca do Rio, leading to Killimane, is dry when the Zambesi is low; but there is always plenty of water in passing Mazaro to the sea, by way of the Luavo mouths.

Above Boca do Rio, on the left hand ascending the river, immediately opposite Mazaro, is Shupanga, where the Zambesi is, both during the wet and also the dry season, at least two miles wide.

On the right hand going up (the left bank of the river), from Boca do Rio to the Rio Shire, the land is called Magangha. The Rio Shire, in the rainy season, has as large a volume of water as the Zambesi; and at the Boca do Shire (or mouth of this river) the Zambesi rises very high in the rainy season, which causes the water at Mazaro to flow down to Killimane, and enables one to enter the Zambesi by that mouth during the whole period of its affluent, the Shire, being in flood; at the other season, as already stated, the Killimane branch is dry, and its bed may be observed at Boca do Rio to be some eight or ten feet higher than the surface of the water in the river during the dry season.

Even in the dry season the Rio Shire is navigable, but the stream is not so rapid as in the Zambesi. The natives ascend it in large canoes, making voyages of from twelve to twenty days, to trade with a people called Magengheros. This river flows past the western flank of the Merambala Mountains (that is to say, these mountains are to the east of it), which are very high. In ascending the Zambesi, this ridge is seen first from Mangara, and it is in sight until after passing Seña.

With reference to the navigation of this affluent of the Zambesi, Dr. Livingstone states, in a letter from Tete, dated Feb. 19, 1859, to Sir George Grey, the great Governor of the Cape Colony:—

"I may mention that we went up the Shire about the beginning of January, and found it a good navigable river for at least a hundred miles from its confluence. The mountain Merambala is four thousand feet high, and has a wonderfully well cultivated large top. Lemon trees grow quite wild in the woods, and so do oranges and pine-apples. There are several fine little fountains, with water slightly chalybeate; the people independent, and very hospitable. The view from the top of the Shire, winding across an extended plain, inhabited by real Solophagi, is magnificent; and, as you may judge from the height, we had quite a different climate from that of the plain. The vegetation is very like that of Loanda and Angola. We have also a fine hot sulphureous fountain at the base (174). Yet no advantage has been taken of this splendid sanatorium by the Portuguese. The valley of the Shire at one part abounds in elephants, and if you come to see us about January, I undertake to show five hundred of these animals grazing in one plain. We saw more than that; as there are branches of the river which form islands, we sometimes chased them with this vessel. They had magnificent tusks. I think that they were attracted down from the hills by the sweet fruit of wild palmyras ,of which there are fine forests there.

"The people are very suspicious of us—never having been visited by Europeans before—but treated us civilly. Our wooding parties were never molested, yet a guard was set over us both *day* and *night*. They are well armed with bows and poisoned arrows. The women insert an ornament exactly the size and shape of the rings for table napkins, into the upper lip. The effect is frightful. It is a most unaccountable ornament. They cultivate largely on the upper third of the Shire valley, and we purchased abundance of provisions at a cheap rate, besides specimens of their cotton yarn. They have two kinds of cotton, and both very good in quality.

"Our first object was to gain their confidence, and seeing them so suspicious, though we had pretty certain information of the Shire becoming smooth again beyond the cataract which stopped our progress, and that Arabs from Zanzibar were in the habit of coming down in canoes from Lake Nyanja, we thought it imprudent to leave the vessel in their power, and go overland. We leave them, to allow our first visit to have its effect, and in the course of a month return to them again. The reason why the Portuguese have not gone farther up about Merambala is, probably, the steady rapidity of the current—two and a half knots. There are no still reaches, and with the heavy Zambesi canoes, it is difficult to get on in a current. The people, too, have had a bad name. They are said to have killed some native traders. In 1856, when I was coming down past the mouth of the Shire, I was told that an expedition had been sent up, but was unable to go far because the river was blocked up with duckweed. Quantities of that were then coming out of the river; but at twenty-five miles from the confluence the duckweed ceases, so that the expedition could not have gone far. Above that the river widens a little, but it is free from sandbanks, and deep. Indeed, it may be said to be superior to the Zambesi for steam navigation. We could get on at night even."

Here we find the intrepid explorer, Dr. Livingstone, opening the Shire to navigation, and determined to reach its source in the Nyngesi, out of which, I was informed by Moors, that river flows to the harbour of Mozambique, and also to

Angoxa. And yet we shall find that when he has accomplished this great feat, a Portuguese minister will spring up and claim the honour of prior discovery for some Canareen who never existed.

On ascending the Zambesi, before arriving at the mouth of the river Shire, one meets with many small islands which have no names, and which disappear during a very wet season; but close to the Boca do Shire, and just below it, are two considerable islands, the first of which is called Ilha Muinha; the second, which is larger, is called Ilha Mozambique, and has about three hundred natives living on it. Ilha Muinha (in Kaffir) means "Salt Island;" and on this island, at Caia, and at Sone (close to Seña), the salt used by those living on the banks of the river is made. Along both banks of the Zambesi the salt is made thus:—A portion of earth (taken up any where) is placed in an earthen vessel with a crack in the bottom of it; this is placed over another vessel, water is poured into the upper vessel, and the earth is moved about; the water that comes through the upper into the lower one is boiled, or allowed to evaporate in the sun; the residuum is very fine salt, proving that the valley of the Zambesi was formerly the bed of the ocean. The country in the interior, opposite the mouth of the Rio Shire, is called Chiringoma, from which to Sofala is eight days' journey, and by land to Seña, twelve days' journey.

After passing the Boca do Shire, and on the opposite side of the Zambesi, is Caia, where the best fish in the river abound; the fish are salted and dried in the sun; some are also smoked, but the former are preferred in the native markets. From Caia to Seña is two days' walking (about ten leagues); by water about three and a half days' (sixteen leagues). After passing Caia, you immediately come to Inhamudendundo, meaning, in the Maravi language, "large country." It runs along the river about five leagues, when one arrives at Inhamatuze, which, in the Seña language, means "dirty island," as in the rainy season it is entirely surrounded by water, at which season, before it was brought under cultivation, it was the resort of numerous animals, who made their lairs there;—it is one league from Seña.

Above the Boca do Shire, on the same side of the river, and nearly opposite to Inhamudendundo, is Santa Beze, in the rear of which, and all the way from the Boca do Shire, is a range of low, rocky mountains, dividing the streams of the Zambesi and Shire, the latter river running between this range and the Merambala Mountains.

Between Seña and Tete there are numerous islands and banks, and even some rocks, and a few eddies; but when the river is in flood, there is no difficulty in the way of steam navigation; and the river may be confined into a narrow channel, at some of the shoaler places, so as to have at all times a channel for navigation.

The Zambesi, even in the dry season, is navigable from the Luavo Mouth to the rapids of Kaord Vasa, for a vessel drawing four feet. During the rainy season, the water rises about sixty feet in the narrows of Lupata, when the rapids of Kaord Vasa are entirely covered, and only require a powerful steamer to overcome them, as Livingstone has just reported. At the same season it will be found that the two rapids above Kaord Vasa will also be navigable; so that the steamer may soon be lying opposite the city of Zumbo, where one of the affluents, or branches, of the Zambesi will give it access to the country of the Cazembe, and even to Londa. Behold what the energy of one Englishman can do! But to carry out this great feat, leading to incalculable benefits to Africa, Livingstone must be provided with a proper steam launch, fitted with a screw (as proposed by me for the exploration of the river Niger, in 1852), instead of the trumpery paddle-wheeled "Ma Robert," very properly designated by Livingstone the "Asthmatic," in allusion to her shortcomings.

As I have already stated, the tide in the Zambesi reaches Mangara. The current is from two to six miles per hour, according to the season. The river is about 3,000 yards wide at Tete; at Seña, 1½ miles; at Killimane, about 800 yards; at Killimane Bar, more than 2 miles; and at the Luavo Mouths, from 200 yards to nearly a mile.

There are no fords. In some dry seasons there are rapids between Seña and Tete; they are always passable. The bed of the river is mud, gravel, and sand.

In the dry season, the water of the river is clear and transparent; in the rainy season, it is brown, and at times approaching to a bright yellow. At this season, the Mozambique Channel is discoloured at a distance of 80 or 100 miles from the Killimane Bar.

In the neighbourhood of Tete, gold, coal, and iron are found in close proximity. Dr. Livingstone has worked the "Asthmatic" with the coal of the country; and he states, in a letter to Sir George Grey, dated Tete, December 18, 1858, that "the Geologist reports having found three seams of coal:—1st, seven feet thick; 2nd, thirteen feet, six inches; 3rd, twenty-five feet thick in a fine cliff section. It was fired by lightning a few years ago, and burned a long time."

Opposite to Tete the country is almost overrun by the sugar-cane. The natives make sugar, but it is of an inferior quality, owing to their not understanding the manufacture of it.

Dr. Livingstone is supplied with a small steam engine, for the purpose of showing the natives in the interior what machinery can do. By the last accounts he had erected this little steam-engine, with which he had sawn timber into planks; and intended trying his hand at making sugar as soon as the cane was fit to cut.

Large quantities of wheat are grown at Tete and in the surrounding country, which is considered the granary of the Zambesi, and may become that of Southern Africa; both Seña and Killimane are already supplied by Tete, which exports 6000 Portuguese bushels of wheat. Any quantity of this wheat may be raised at six shillings per quarter.

The people of Tete have a great advantage over other parts of the river, for in the rear of the town, and only a mile distant from it, is the Karuera, a high mountain, said to be from 3,000 to 5,000 feet in height. Here they have their plantations, consisting of different varieties of Indian or Kaffir corn, peas, beans, sweet potatoes, cabbages, onions, &c.; and close to the village is a place called Ilhalutanda, having an area of from ten to twenty square miles, which, in the rainy season, is more or less flooded. When the waters retire, they plant rice, corn, wheat, beans, &c.; so that, should the plantations in the high lands fail for want of rain, they have a crop below; and if the floods destroy the crop below, they have a supply in the mountains. In the rainy season, there is generally a great fall of rain, accompanied by very high winds from the south and south-west.

At times, when it is very hot, after continued calms, they have violent whirlwinds, which destroy everything in their course, breaking trees, and taking up houses, and whirling them in the air as if they were straw mats. Some years, in the months of June and July, they have a hot wind from the south-west, which burns up everything that may be in the ground; but this is unusual.

From Inhasuja (which is close to Killimane) to Mazaro, and even in different parts of the river, as high as Seña, the natives build their huts on stakes, about twenty feet above the ground, so that in the rainy season they will not be endangered by the floods, which are constant and sudden. During this time it is not unusual for a native to indulge in the luxury of fishing out of his bed. In 1855, thousands of the natives were drowned by the river rising higher than usual; many who escaped the flood fell victims to the famine that succeeded it.

Fish of different species abound in the Zambesi. Buqueña; a long fish, long head, no scales; white; from one to six feet in length, weighing about eight pounds; very oily, and without any small bones. Pende; from six to twenty inches in length, broad scales, black; from one to four pounds in weight; no small bones. Muja; from one to six feet in length; long scales; round head, sides silver, back black; from one to ten pounds in weight. Cação; shark, called in the salt water Tuberaõ. Similarly, certain fish of this family ascend the Senegal, Amazon, and other great rivers, to the distance of several hundred miles from the ocean (*vide* Lyell's *Manual of Elementary Geology*, 5th edition, p. 126; and the Proceedings Geol. Soc., No. 43, p. 222). There are many other fish, and none poisonous.

The principal feeders or tributaries of the Zambesi are, the Shire, between Mazaro and Seña, which is now being explored by Dr. Livingstone; the Zangué, just below Seña (it is small); the Aruenha, between Massangane and Marangue; the Revubue, nearly opposite to Tete, besides the Loangwa, the Luambesi, and a host of others above the rapids of Kaord Vasa.

The banks of the river are well wooded with large timber; many varieties of which are well-adapted for ship-building, and all for household furniture and cabinet purposes.

The timber is to be found close to the stream. In the dry season it may be cut down, hewn into logs, placed on the banks of the river, and there formed into rafts, which, with the rising waters, could be easily navigated to the various mouths of the river, and supply the increasing wants of this country for ship-building timber. Here, as on the west coast of the same continent, side by side with the heavy teak wood, whose specific gravity is so great that it will barely float, and even sometimes sinks in the water, may be found the cork-wood tree, wherewith to float the heavy timber to the shipping.

See the Appendix A, for a list of *Medicinal*

Botanical trees, herbs, and plants, and some of the uses to which they are put by the natives.

A list of woods to be found on the Zambesi, specimens of which were brought home by me, and are to be seen at the rooms of the Royal Geographical Society, will be found in Appendix B.

CHAPTER XII.

Angoxa—Its History—Perfidious Conduct of the Portuguese—Effects of British Interference—Wholesale Dread which the Portuguese have of the Imâm of Muskat—Visit of the Sultan of Angoxa to Johanna—Invites a British Merchant to Trade with him—Seizure of the British Brig "Reliance."

PASSING on from the mouths of the Zambesi, with all its untold treasures, we come to a country which, having abandoned the slave-trade, and entered into legitimate commerce, finds its reward in growing richer and more powerful every year, while the neighbouring Portuguese settlements, abandoned to the nefarious traffic in human beings, become annually more impoverished.

Steaming along this coast the prospect was quite enchanting, as ever and anon island after island rose from the sea, displaying their shores of the purest white sand, surrounded by the blue ocean, and surmounted by the beautiful and graceful Kasurina tree, which, at a distance, has much the appearance of our own fir tree.

At last we anchored as close as the surrounding reef would permit us, to an island called Mafamale.

This island is at the mouth of the Angoxa river, and is well known to the Arabs who frequent these seas as the burial-place of one of their prophets.

We visited the island, and made diligent search for the tomb of the prophet, but could not find a vestige of anything which might be taken for an Arab tomb. In fact, the only marks which we observed at all on the island of its having been visited at any time, were that some of the trees had been lately cut down and removed; and we also saw the remains of a recent fire.

On the 15th of July, the morning after we anchored, the Prime Minister of the Sultan of Angoxa came on board the "Hermes," accompanied by the Sultan's nephew. The latter evidently came to look after the prime minister, who, although entirely in the confidence of the chief of the country, was anxious to get back to Zanzibar, of which place he was one of the Arab community.

On the following day Captain Gordon went up the river and paid a visit to the Sultan, at the town of Angoxa, which is situated at the distance of twelve miles from the mouth of the river; to which there are two entrances, so that a vessel may enter and go out with a fair wind in either monsoon.

The town of Angoxa consists of a number of small houses, built partly of stone and partly of wood, the roofs being of the leaves of the palm or cocoa-nut. It contains about 1,000 inhabitants, the greater part of whom are Arabs, and carries on a considerable trade with the Arab settlements at Zanzibar, Melinda, and Mombas.

Angoxa supplies immense quantities of simsim, or sesame, or guergelin seed (which appears here particularly to thrive), the oil expressed from which is a valuable article of commerce, being used as a substitute for olive oil, and much prized for the finer portions of machinery.

Ivory in abundance, ebony, orchella weed, gum copal, cocoa-nut oil, coir and ground nuts form the principal portions of cargoes of fleets of dhows trading, in the season, between this country and the dominions of the Imãm of Muskat.

The Sultan of Angoxa, who is an independant prince, asks for a British consular agent, and is anxious to place himself under the protection of Great Britain; meanwhile the Mozambique government threatens the seizure of English vessels trading with Angoxa.

The kingdom of Angoxa extends at present from Sliangazi, at the mouth of Captain Owen's river Antonio, about twenty miles to the northward of Angoxa river, whilst the southern limit is Quizano or Moma, about sixty or seventy miles from the mouth of the same river. By this it will be seen that it has a seaboard of ninety miles; while I was informed that the Angoxa river is navigated about sixty leagues, or 180 miles, from its mouth. Over the whole of the country through which that portion of the Angoxa river runs, which is navigated at present, the Sultan of

Angoxa is acknowledged as the supreme head, having under his rule from thirty to forty chiefs, more or less powerful.

The Angoxa river is said to take its rise in a large lake. This may be the lake Maravi, which, from what I learned from the Moors at Mozambique, has an outlet by a river discharging itself either at Angoxa or Mozambique.

The history of Angoxa is contained in the following statement, derived from reliable sources:—

At one time the government of that Arabic kingdom was located at Killimane, a place much desired by the Portuguese, as it commands one of the mouths of the Zambesi. About fourteen Sultans' reigns since, negotiations were entered into by the authorities at the island of Mozambique, with the then reigning Sultan of the kingdom of Angoxa, at the capital, Killimane, for the purchase of that town. Terms were agreed upon; and, in order that there should be no misunderstanding, the Sultan removed to the river Angoxa. A yearly tribute, or rent, was to be paid by the Portuguese to the Sultan for the use of Killimane. Eight Sultans received this tribute money. The ninth Sultan went for a number of years to the city of Mozambique and received this rent, but after some time the Portuguese pleaded inability to pay, and asked for time, which was granted by the Sultan. After a number of years, having always received the same messages from Mozambique, he determined to go in person and demand the rent which was in arrear. Arrived at Mozambique, he found a new Governor-general, who ignored the Killimane arrangement, and on the other hand demanded from the Sultan of Angoxa tribute-money, due by him as a vassal to the King of Portugal, and which he claimed as being in arrear the same number of years that the Mozambique government had omitted paying the rent for Killimane.

The Sultan of Angoxa, taken by surprise, was imprisoned at Mozambique; a member of his family was found willing to reign over Angoxa as Sultan, acknowledging himself as the vassal of the King of Portugal, and from that time Angoxa was claimed as a Portuguese possession. The Portuguese Sultan, in consequence of murdering a member of his own family, was driven out of Angoxa by his subjects. A new Sultan was set up by one party, while the cause of another claimant to the throne was advocated by a second party at Angoxa. The latter repaired to Mozambique, and with the assistance of the government of that place, and his own adherents at Angoxa, was created Sultan of Angoxa, subject again to the authorities at Mozambique. Soon after being placed in the government, he was dethroned, and was succeeded by others who did not acknowledge the sovereignty of Portugal; and this state of affairs continued until the attention of the British government having been called by the Portuguese to the slave-trade at Angoxa, Commodore Wyvill was instructed to put a stop to it; and having, I am informed, called upon the Portuguese authorities at Mozambique to assist him in coercing their so-called rebellious subjects at Angoxa, an attack was made by Her Majesty's naval, and the Portuguese small military, force. The Sultan of Angoxa promised to abandon the slave-trade, and was forced to acknowledge the sovercignty of Portugal.

A fiscal officer was placed on the point of land

at the mouth of the river. As soon as he was unprotected, the natives of Angoxa forced him to take to the boat which had been left with him to escape by (for such an event was fully expected), and so ends for the last time the sovereignty of Portugal over Angoxa.

It must not for a moment be imagined that the assistance of Commodore Wyvill was solicited by the Portuguese authorities for the purpose of stopping the slave-trade; that was simply the pretext by which they obtained the assistance of the senior British naval officer to force upon the Angoxa people their hated rule. For I know, from persons who were then resident at Mozambique, that the slave-trade was at that time flourishing in Mozambique harbour, and that a Spanish slaver was lying off Inhambane for more than three weeks, waiting for slaves, during which time she was supplied by the authorities at that place, and went away with 1000 slaves. It is in this manner that the British government has been duped, and British officers have been made instruments for extending the Portuguese dominion, under the specious pretext of stopping the slave-trade, which would have been more effectually done if the Portuguese had been left to maintain their sovereignty where they were able to do so; and, at all other parts of the coast, a system of open ports and free trade had been established.

The Portuguese government, having obtained from Great Britain an acknowledgment of its sovereignty over the coast from Cape Delgado to Delagoa Bay, insists on maintaining it, although it does not carry out the terms of the agreement, viz.:—The abolition of the slave-trade in the province of Mozambique. The faithless are always most exacting in faith from others.

The Angoxa people know the Portuguese as the nation who once oppressed them, and perfidiously deprived them of Killimane, the capital of their kingdom, situated on a mouth of the river Zambesi, the great commercial highway of Eastern Africa.

The Sultan of Angoxa asks for a consular officer from England, and trades with the subjects of the Imâm of Muskat. I have seen dhows belonging to Zanzibar, with cargoes from Angoxa, on their return from that place to Zanzibar, anchor within gun-shot of the fort of Mozambique, during a calm, or for a whole night, and resume their voyage without being interrupted by the authorities at Mozambique; so much do the latter dread their neighbour, the Imâm of Muskat, whose plain red Arab flag these dhows fly. The reason for this is that on the Sultan of Angoxa driving away the fiscal officer placed there by the Portuguese when assisted by the British, under Commodore Wyvill, he offered to place himself under the protection of the Imâm of Muskat, but the Imâm refused the offer made by the Sultan of Angoxa, fearing to offend the English. At the same time, he sent an intimation to the Governor-general of Mozambique, once and for ever, that if he found him interfering, in any way, with the trade established between Angoxa and Zanzibar, or molesting any dhow or vessel with his flag flying on her, he would come with his ships and blow the city of Mozambique into the water, before England or France could come to its assistance. The Portuguese knew him well, and what he was capable of doing. He had taken from them Mombas and Melinda, and they wished to retain the last monument of their glory in the kingdom of Algarves; the consequence is that, as I have already related, the Portuguese do not interfere in the lucrative trade carried on by the Arabs of Zanzibar. On the other hand, any vessel with the British flag, trading at Angoxa, is immediately seized and plundered. I state facts, which I defy the Mozambique people or the Portuguese government to deny. Now to the proof.

In the year 1851 or 1852, the Sultan of Angoxa paid a visit to the Sultan of Johanna, one of the Comoro Islands, and while residing there made the acquaintance of an English merchant settled at that island. He informed the English merchant of a fact, viz., that he was an independent Sultan, most anxious to trade with the English. He told him of the riches of his country; how that from Angoxa, the simsim, or sesame, or guergelin seed, (the oil of which vies with that of the olive) is taken in great quantities to Zanzibar, and thence to Europe; how fleets of dhows are engaged, during the trading season, between Angoxa and Zanzibar. He described to him the ebony and beautiful figured woods of the country; the wax in abundance; tortoise shells and ivory, and, in fact, did all in his power to induce the merchant to visit him. The merchant, sometime afterwards, having occasion to go in his vessel to Mozambique, called in at Angoxa to see the Sultan, and make arrangements for future trading. I believe no trading transactions took place. The vessel weighed and left the river, outside of which was lying a small Portuguese schooner-of-war. As soon as the English vessel was beyond the protection of the Sultan, and out of gun-shot distance from the shore, and, consequently, out of the territory of the sovereign of the country, whether the Sultan of Angoxa or the King of Portugal, the small Portuguese schooner-of-war ranged alongside of the English vessel, and ordered her to keep company to the port of Mozambique. The merchant, a man of law and order, hailed to reply that he was going there. They sailed in company together, and when they arrived in the harbour of Mozambique, the Englishman discovered that he was a prisoner, his vessel was confiscated, and to this hour he has obtained no redress.

The name of the vessel which was thus seized was the "Reliance," a brig under English colours; and the merchant was Mr. William Sunley, residing at Johanna, one of the Comoro Islands, and at present Her Majesty's consul at that island. On referring to that gentleman, I think it will be found that I have stated the circumstances very fairly.

On Captain Gordon's return to the "Hermes," the anchor was weighed; and, although there was a present of a bullock from the Sultan to the captain, and another to myself, besides quantities of fowls on the way down the river, we could not wait for them, but steamed away to Mozambique, our arrival at which will form the subject of the next chapter.

CHAPTER XIII.

Arrival at Mozambique — Interview with the Governor-general—Saluting the Consular Flag —Description of the Consul's House on the Mainland—Portuguese Rosa—Cruelty of the Portuguese Towards their Slaves—"Flog until he will Require no More"—Irrigation and Native Labour.

On the 18th of July, 1857, H.M.S. "Hermes" arrived at Mozambique; the harbour master paid his visit; the Portuguese flag on the Fort was saluted with twenty-one guns; and the Governor-general's *aide-de-camp*, a nephew of the Sa de Bandeira, came on board to inform me that His Excellency and his lady would receive myself and my lady at eleven o'clock the next day.

In order to be punctual, shortly before the appointed hour, Captain Gordon, Mrs. M'Leod, and myself, accompanied by Mr. Soares, who had kindly consented to act as interpreter, left the side of the "Hermes" in Captain Gordon's gig. As soon as the boat was clear off the ship's guns, the "Hermes" fired a consular salute, which was immediately taken up by Fort San Sebastian.

We landed on the handsome and substantially-built wharf, which will be referred to when describing the city of Mozambique, on which a large number of negroes were collected, and a few Portuguese.

In waiting, there was a description of palanquin, borne by four negroes, which the Governor-general had, with marked attention, sent "for the use of the English Señhora, to screen her from the gaze of the rude blacks." Thanks were returned for the courteous offer, but my wife, preferring to walk with her husband, the palanquin was not put in requisition. While walking along the pier, on our way to the palace, the scabbard came off my sword, without being noticed by me, and the first intimation I had of the accident was on its being presented to me, in a very graceful manner, by a young slave. A trifle, which is not worth mentioning, but which the slave-dealers of

Mozambique spoke of as an omen of what the British consul was going to do, and is simply alluded to as showing how the merest trifle is seized upon by these degraded men with superstitious dread.

At the inner end of the pier, on the right hand side, is a large square building, coloured pink, having a sentinel on guard in front of it: this is the Mozambique Custom-house, and from the thickness of the walls it is the coolest place in the whole town.

Passing the Custom-house, we approached the Palace, which was coloured on the outside partly white and partly pink, giving to it a very pleasing appearance, and entered by an archway which led us to a court-yard in the centre of the Palace, whence the entrance to the public rooms was approached by a double flight of steps, on ascending which we were received by the *aides-de-camp*, ushered into the reception-room, and requested to be seated.

In about five minutes' time, a tall, thin, nervous-looking man, with intelligence stamped upon his brow, was ushered into the room by the *aides-de-camp*—this was Vasco Guedes e Carvelhos de Menezes, Governor-general of Mozambique. We had evidently been too punctual; and His Excellency's anxiety not to keep us waiting, together with his half-finished toilet, added much to the natural nervousness of his manner. He was accompanied by a gentleman, whose soft, cat-like motion, clean shaved face, white linen, neatly fitted garments, scrupulously clean hands, dark piercing eyes, and white teeth, so large and so even—so fully shown when he smiled—the whole completed by a voice whose tone was melody, spoke at once the polished gentleman and the self-possessed Jesuit. This gentleman was His Excellency's secretary.

Having presented the Exequatur of Don Pedro the Fifth, by the Grace of God, King of Portugal and the Algarves, on this side and the other of the sea round Africa, Lord of Guinea, and of the Conquest, the Navigation and Commerce of Ethiopia, Arabia, Persia, and of India, &c., it was handed to the secretary for registration in the archives of the province, and we began to converse.

Captain Gordon at once stated the circumstances under which he had fired at the Portuguese schooner of war "Zambesi," off the mouth of the Inhambane river, and expressed his regret that in consequence of the obstinacy of the commander of that vessel, in not heaving-to nor showing his colours, he was obliged to have recourse to measures which might have led to serious consequences. The Governor-general accepted the explanation most graciously, and the secretary smiled. That smile said, "I know all about it." And I found afterwards that he was aware, even then when we were speaking, although the "Zambesi" had not arrived in harbour, that at the time the "Hermes" fired at the "Zambesi" Ex-Governor Leotti was a passenger in her, and was on his way to the Bazarutto Islands, after his unsuccessful attempt to usurp the government of Inhambane, for the purpose of supplying the "Minnetonka" slaver, under American colours, and bound for Havannah de Cuba with a cargo of slaves.

The mentioning of the "Zambesi" affair led the Governor-general to ask if we had seen any suspicious-looking vessel on our way up the Mozambique Channel, upon which the name of the "Minnetonka" was mentioned, and the circumstances under which she visited Port Natal, and also that we had been informed that her destination was Cape Corrientes, better known as Inhambane. The Governor-general assured us that she would not obtain one slave from Cape Delgado to Delagoa Bay; that the traffic had entirely ceased; that the Mozambique people were entirely opposed to the slave-trade; that they had turned their attention to legitimate commerce; and, now that the British consul had arrived, he hoped to see him followed by British vessels, when the marvellous commercial resources of the province would be developed. He referred to his secretary, who confirmed all His Excellency stated with a bland smile. Madam Guedes, the Governor-general's wife, now entered, and the conversation turned to other subjects. She gave us both a most hearty welcome to her house, though she would not add it to a climate in which she had suffered much, and from the effects of which she appeared to be slowly recovering. She was accompanied by her child, a girl of three years old, born at Mozambique, who looked indeed a tender plant.

Even in this first interview, I could not but contrast the appearance of everything at the Palace with the description given by Salt of his reception at Mozambique, about fifty years since, as may be seen by the following statement :—

"After dinner we retired to another apartment, where tea and coffee were set out in a splendid service of pure gold from Seña, of excellent workmanship, executed by the Banians resident on the island. The Governor, when in his official dress, wears a very costly and curiously wrought chain of the same metal, and, on state days, has two or three black slaves in attendance, who appear almost overwhelmed by the pressure of the golden ornaments with which they are encumbered, remnants of the splendour once attending these viceroys of Eastern Africa."

The gold chain of office here alluded to has been appropriated by some predecessor of Vasco Guedes, and the golden tea and coffee service must have shared the same fate, as the present Mozambiquers have no knowledge of such articles having existed; while those of their slaves who are covered have barely sufficient of the commonest material to hide their nakedness.

Having taken leave of His Excellency and family, we walked about the town, and were conducted to Mr. Soares' house, where his father, the Brigadier Candido de Costa Soares, was introduced to us.

It was arranged, at the Cape of Good Hope, that a large house in the city of Mozambique, belonging to Mr. Soares, was to be leased to me. But on our arrival we found that Mr. Soares' instructions had not been complied with in his absence, for the repairs which were to have been made previous to his return were not even commenced. It was found quite impossible to procure any other house on the island, even with the assistance of the Governor-general; and, although bitterly disappointed at this unexpected occurrence relative to a residence in the city, Mr. Soares having assured me that we should find his house there quite prepared, and at my disposal, I was obliged to content myself with that gentleman's solemn assurance that the house would be immediately put into a state of repair, and that, as soon as that was done, one-half of the house would become mine for twelve months. The house was a very large one, divided into two distinct portions by a massive double stone staircase, and I found that one half of it would have been quite large enough for my purpose. Meanwhile it was arranged, as an earnest of Mr. Soares' sincerity (who appeared much mortified that his instructions had not been complied with during his absence), that the British consular flag should be hoisted on the flag-staff which was already erected on the house; and that until the portion of the building required for my use was ready for occupation, I should have the use of Mr. Soares' house on the mainland.

The following day was devoted to hoisting the consular flag, and opening the British Consulate. The Union Jack was accordingly hoisted at noon, and saluted by the Fort with twenty-one guns, which was acknowledged by a similar salute from H.M.S.V. "Hermes." In the evening, the captain, and a number of the officers from the "Hermes," together with myself, were entertained at dinner; Mrs. M'Leod, from slight indisposition, not being able to attend.

Next morning, at daylight, we left the "Hermes," exchanging the kind and unbounded hospitality shown us by Captain Gordon, R.N. for the quiet of our own home in East Africa.

The house to which we were conducted, and in which we were to suffer so much, was on the N.W. end of Mozambique Harbour, built on the beach, and about a stone's throw above high water mark.

In front of it, and looking towards the island of Mozambique, there was an extensive sandy beach, which, at low water, in full and change of the tides, was uncovered for the space of about two and a half miles; so that, at those periods, one could walk over the sands to within about half a mile of the island. At other times, the sand-bank was more or less, according to the state of the tide, covered with water. Along the beach, and at high water mark, a few mangrove trees marked the unhealthy character of the location.

The house itself was a large, square, solid-looking building, with a flat roof. It was surrounded by a wall, some ten or twelve feet in height, which enclosed a space covering about an acre of ground, and within which there was a kitchen, outhouses for the slaves, and a stable having accommodation for three horses.

The chambers on the basement were large and lofty, but were only used as store-rooms.

On the floor above there was one large sitting or reception-room, and three other apartments; access to which was obtained from the front of the house by a door on the basement, leading to a massive stone staircase; and on the rear of the house, by a double stone staircase leading from the court-yard.

The spaces for windows of the rooms on the basement were barred by iron wood; the door of the house was double and folding, and all the fastenings were heavy, awkward, and cumbersome, evidently made with a view to resist any attacks of the natives. The windows of the upper apartments were one half glass, and the other half a wooden shutter on hinges, which opened to admit air; while the glass part was fitted with a similar shutter to exclude, when necessary, the intense light of that latitude.

The reception-room was furnished with two light Indian sofas, which looked cool and inviting; a dozen and a half chairs, of all descriptions, collected from every quarter of the globe, each design showing that comfort was the object sought; three tables placed conveniently in the apartment; a few good French coloured prints on the wall; a number of books in English, French, Portuguese, Spanish, and Italian, on a variety of subjects—history, architecture, agriculture, mining, poetry, and *belles-lettres*—scattered about the room, showed the attainments of the owner. In one corner stood two barometers, one French and the other English, while close adjoining, on the wall, hung an aneroid. In another part of the room was seen one of Dent's duplidescopes for finding noon by the double reflection of the meridian sun in any latitude; by its side a German microscope, and a French alarm clock. Exploring the next apartment, one came across a magic lantern, Chinese puzzles carved in ivory, and a complete apparatus for the Daguerreotype process. These all attested to the various tastes of the owner, and it was his favourite boast that the house contained everything; in proof of which, on visiting the store-room below, he showed me a rusty rat-trap, an American cotton-gin, palms and needles, copal varnish, rockets; and, in short, anything that I named was, as if by enchantment, immediately produced.

The house, with the slaves attached to it, twenty-three in number, and a small open carriage with one horse, were at my service, and to be considered absolutely mine for twelve months; the rent to be agreed upon as soon as a kitchen was built adjoining the house, so as to cook in it in the English style; and the sum was agreed upon which the rent was not to exceed.

Mr. Soares had breakfast prepared, and bade us welcome, saying that he was glad to show us some return for our kindness to him "when, sick and lonely at the Cape of Good Hope, we nursed and made him well."

The ollowing day our baggage was landed from the "Hermes," and she proceeded to sea some days afterwards.

Mr. Soares had asked me as a favour to allow a widow woman, who had acted as overseer to the slaves in the house, to remain and take charge of the slaves; and my wife was delighted to have some one who knew how to manage them, and was glad to show the poor widow some kindness. But before two days Mrs. M'Leod was obliged to speak to her for her cruel treatment of the negroes, and begged her to be more gentle with them for the future. In the evening, when going out for a drive, the Portuguese woman told them to take the horse out of the carriage, and informed her mistress that she was placed there to take care of Mr. Soares' slaves and property. I was obliged to tell Mr. Soares that neither as an Englishman, nor a British consul, could I allow any slave to be treated as Portuguese Rosa had used them in my presence; and as only one woman could command in an Englishman's house, the poor widow, who did not understand her position, must go. He explained her conduct by stating that she behaved herself in that manner on purpose to be sent to his plantation in the country, where she would command everybody. The next day she left the house, and great was the rejoicing of the slaves when she was gone.

When we took the house, the slaves, with the exception of one who was a carpenter, and appeared to be a favourite with Portuguese Rosa, were, without exception, the most miserable, broken-hearted looking negroes I ever saw. They had the appearance of having been half-starved for a very long period, and were covered with scars and sores, evidently the effects of brutal treatment. One poor creature was so horrifying a sight, that I asked Mr. Soares if it was not possible to do something to alleviate his sufferings, when he was sent to the house of Mr. Soares' father to be treated by the slave doctor there. He begged me not to think his slaves were in that condition always; and accounted for it by his absence from Mozambique, stating that, when he returned after an absence of any duration, he was sure to find that some of his slaves were dead, and many of them had run away into the Makua country; which he felt certain was caused by the cruel treatment of those whom he had left in charge of them. He added that he rejoiced they were with me, for now there would be an end of this, as far as those who were attached to this house of his. I observed, on his making his appearance among them, that they clapped their hands, as if glad at his presence; but I found no expression of this feeling in their countenances; and I soon learned that they made this clapping of their hands on seeing me, or my wife, or, in fact, any one with a white face—and that it was not only their glorious privilege to be slaves, but that they had to express their joy in this manner on beholding their oppressors. How abject must be that domestic slavery which degrades the image of God to such baseness!

However, we set about improving their condition gradually. Owing to the poor food, and scanty allowance of it, which was served out to them, their blood was very much impoverished, and their bodies were covered with disgusting running sores; the fingers and toes of some of the younger slaves being almost rotted off—and in this condition their oppressors expected them to perform their daily task. The appearance of some was really too horrible to be described. I ordered sulphur and lard to be applied, and had to superintend the treatment myself, as the elder ones could not be persuaded at first to assist their younger fellow-sufferers. They were induced to bathe in the salt water morning and evening. At first there was some difficulty about the matter, but by dint of a little coaxing the elder ones took to it, and then there was no difficulty with the younger ones. The allowance of food was really not sufficient to sustain life, consisting entirely of a description of small grain called milho. This allowance was served out about once a week; a day more or less seemed to be a matter of indifference. The food served out in this manner to the poor hungry negroes was of course seized upon with avidity, and what was intended for a week's supply seldom lasted for more than two or three days, and on the fourth day all were crying for food. Until the end of the week they had no chance of receiving any from their own masters; they must, therefore, rob them, or some other person; when found out, they were flogged. Hunger was ever goading them on to rob; the lash was always ready, and therefore the whip was always going.

If found stealing cocoa-nuts from the trees, the custom of Mozambique is to allow the captain or guardian of the palm trees to shoot them. No question is asked as to how a slave comes by his death—and the body is thrown into the sea.

The reason for giving them so little food is not that their masters are unable to feed them, but simply that they come of a fierce race, and it is necessary to keep them in subjection. The Portuguese are always dreading their slaves rising upon them; and, therefore, they exercise all their ingenuity in devising means to keep them down, and display a refinement in cruelty which I am not aware exists in any other slave-holding communities. Here at Mozambique, where slaves are plentiful, and where there is no difficulty in replacing them, they are not valued as in those places where a human being represents so many thousand dollars, or hundred doubloons. Here a slave is only worth forty dollars, even when the slave ships from Réunion or Cuba lie in the harbour. If a slave is refractory, and flogging only makes him worse, the arbitrary master, enraged at his continued disobedience, bids his brutal overseer flog him until "he will require no more." The master looks on and gloats his vengeance. The slave perishes under the lash—a few dollars will replace him. Not so where he cannot be replaced except at considerable expense. This is one thing which peculiarly aggravates the domestic slavery of Mozambique, viz., the facility with which the negro is replaced. To keep them in subjection, every opportunity is seized to destroy all sympathy with each other, and all natural affection. The son is made to flog his mother and his sister; the father flogs his daughters, and also the woman who bore them for him—all at the command of their owner, who can do with them what he pleases. Women are made to flog—and that under circumstances too revolting to be told. If two persons of different sexes are observed growing attached to each other, and there is springing up between them that feeling which we would unquestionably call love, but which the proud superiority of the Portuguese intellect denies can exist in men and women with black skins,—those two are chosen for each other's executioners. It is thus that, making nature war against itself, they endeavour to create and perpetuate an unnatural race, destitute of all affection to each other. They war against the Omnipotent—love they cannot eradicate from the human heart—woe to that hour when vengeance wakes to life!

Increased supplies of food were given to the slaves attached to my house; some were supplied with nets, and sent to collect fish, which were to be found in abundance on the beach before the house; all were kept employed. The garden, once a neglected ruin, soon smiled; and the contented, well fed negro laughed aloud. The orange trees, pronounced dead, returned to life, and with their golden fruit rewarded our care. The rose trees, which had been brought from the Brazils when the slave-trade flourished, on our arrival looked like wild briers; but trimmed and trained by Englishwomen, and watered by the slaves, they soon bore roses the size of small dahlias, whose fragrance was astonishing. The barren fig-trees were not ungrateful, and presented us with their cool, luscious fruit every morning. The pomegranate trees dazzled us with the rich carnation colour of their flowers, and their fruit formed an agreeable dessert. The banana and the pine-apple improved so much in flavour, that they were not recognized as Mozambique fruit by those names: the banana tasted more like that of China; and the pine-apple approached the hot-house fruit of that name. When H.M.S.V. "Cordelia" called at Mozambique, on her way to the Kuria Muria Islands, the captain's gig, on her return to the ship, was filled with peas, lettuces, cabbages, and oranges from my garden, until Captain Vernon begged me to put no more in—or else she would sink. This was only a few months after our arrival at Mozambique: showing what irrigation and native labour, properly directed, may do in that climate in a short space of time.

CHAPTER XIV.

Brief Historical Sketch of the Portuguese on the East Coast of Africa—Description of Mozambique—Its Position as an Emporium for Commerce—Its Restoration, like that of Alexandria, possible—Fort San Sebastian—Churches and Chapels—Palace of the Governor-General—Wharf—Population—Society.

TEN years after the discovery of the Cape of Good Hope by Bartholomew Diaz, while Columbus was yet at the height of his glory, and previous to the unmerited ignominy heaped upon that "Great Light of the Age" by ungrateful Spain, Don Emmanuel, King of Portugal, in 1497, despatched Vasco de Gama to follow up the discoveries of his countryman Diaz.

De Gama, having under his command three vessels, manned with sixty men, left Lisbon on the 8th July, 1497. He called at the Cape de Verde Islands, and thence continued his course to the southward, along the coast of Africa, until he came to an anchor in St. Helena Bay. Two days after quitting which, he attained the latitude of the Cape of Good Hope, where he had to contend with the south-east trade-wind, and the insubordination of his crews. Having, by his perseverance and address, overcome the opposition of the elements and the mutineers in his fleet, he rounded the great promontory of Africa, and by his subsequent success, earned for himself the proud distinction, throughout all ages, of having been the first who reached India by that route.

Anxious to visit Sofala, discovered by his countryman Covilham, he followed the coast of Africa from its southern extreme. He anchored in Saint Blasse Bay, after leaving which, he arrived at the island of Santa Cruz, which was the limit of the discoveries of his predecessor Diaz. Thence, continuing his own discoveries, he kept the land in view as he proceeded to the northward. He touched at Natal, passed Sofala, and arrived at Mozambique, where he anchored, according to Osorio, on the 1st of March, but, according to the *Diario Portuguez*, on the 28th February, 1498, just two months before Columbus set out on his third voyage.

De Gama found that Mozambique was an Arab settlement, under the dominion of the Sultan of Kilwa, whose subordinate, Zacoëja, was then governor of Mozambique.

Kilwa was described to him as one of the most celebrated ports of the country, having vessels which had constant commercial relations with Arabia, Persia, and India.

Sofala was spoken of as the country which furnished large and inexhaustible quantities of gold; and he found that the whole trade of the country was in the hands of the Arabs, whose vessels were supplied with the mariner's compass, marine charts, and astrolabes, or instruments for taking the altitude of the heavenly bodies, for the purpose of navigating these seas.

His application for pilots to take him to Calicut was readily complied with, and two pilots were furnished to him by the governor, Zacoëja.

On the arrival of the Portuguese at Mozambique,

it was at first supposed that the strangers were Arab traders from Berbera, on the north-east coast of Africa, opposite to the Arab emporium of Aden, and hence arose the hospitality with which they were received. But on the true state of the case being known, that De Gama and his followers were "infidel dogs," who had found their way from the west round the Cape of Good Hope, the animosity of the Arabs was immediately let loose upon the strangers; who, not satisfied with depriving them of their fair possessions in the west, had circumnavigated Africa, to despoil them in the east.

On this discovery being made, the battle of the Crescent and the Cross commenced in the Indian Ocean, and from that moment De Gama had another difficulty to contend with in his voyage of discovery.

In consequence of the hostility displayed towards him by the Mozambique people, he was obliged to quit the port, and directed his course in search of Kilwa, in order to place himself in communication with the Sultan of that place.

His pilots, doubtless acting under the instructions of the Mozambique Arabs, failed to reach

Kilwa, but, instead, found themselves off Mombas. They endeavoured to persuade De Gama that the greater part of the inhabitants of Mombas were Christians, and that it was the most suitable place to refit his ships, and refresh their crews, after their long and harassing voyage.

These pilots, mixing with the subordinate officers and the crews of the admiral's vessel, laid before them such a pleasant prospect of the scenes of pleasure which awaited them at Mombas, that the Portuguese broke out into that state of mutiny which, in those days, led to the most disastrous results, and frequently frustrated the noblest enterprises.

De Gama was forced to yield to the solicitations of his crews; and, with a presentiment of impending danger, he reluctantly anchored at Mombas.

At Mombas he found the people in a high state of civilization; the princes and chiefs clothed in silk and satin; the city defended by formidable fortresses mounting artillery; and the houses of the inhabitants similar to those in old Spain. In fact, before him lay a Moorish or Arab city, well fortified.

A plan was concocted by the Arabs of Mombas to seize the Portuguese squadron, but being alarmed by some unnatural noise made in the hold of the admiral's ship at the moment when they were about to put their plan into execution, a panic seized the ringleaders, and their untimely flight revealed to De Gama the danger which he had fortunately escaped. He immediately put to sea, and repaired to Melinda, where he was received with great cordiality by the Sheik Wagerage, who sent his son Ali on board of the admiral's ship to bid him welcome, excusing himself from visiting De Gama on account of his great age and infirmities.

Here De Gama was furnished with experienced pilots; and in return for the attentions of the aged Sheik, he promised to call at Melinda on his return from India, and convey to the King of Portugal the ambassadors, whom the Sheik of Melinda expressed his intention of sending for the purpose of making a treaty of friendship and alliance.

On the 22nd of April De Gama left Melinda, and stretching across the Indian Ocean for Calicut, passed the equator, and once more beheld the well-known constellation of the northern hemisphere. On the 28th of May, 1498, thirty-six days after leaving Melinda, the squadron of De Gama anchored at Calicut.

Thus was India reached by way of the Cape of Good Hope, and De Gama realized the dream of Don Henry, conceived eighty-six years before, and left by that prince as a legacy to the enterprise of his countrymen, to whom he had set the example of half a century of persevering energy.

By his prudent conduct De Gama overcame the opposition of the Mahometans, and obtained the favour of the Zamorin of Calicut. After visiting Goâ, the Portuguese squadron put again to sea, traversed the Arabian Gulf, and commenced running down the length of the African coast from north to south.

Passing Mogadoxa, the squadron bombarded that Arab stronghold, destroying many of the houses, and sinking a great number of vessels; evidently with the intention of striking terror into the followers of the Prophet.

True to his promise, De Gama called at Melinda; embarked the ambassadors of the

Sheik, and, after a short stay of five days, proceeded to the island of Zanzibar, arriving there on the 29th April, 1499. There, although occupied by Mahometan Arabs, he was well received; being furnished with live stock, vegetables, and fruit in abundance. Doubtless the fame of his deeds had preceded him, and the wily Arabs of that place wished to avoid making an enemy of one who had the power of visiting them with a severe retribution.

Leaving Zanzibar, he sailed along the Mozambique coast, wisely reserving his chastisement of the Mozambiquers for a future day. He watered his ships at Saint Blasse Bay, doubled the Cape of Good Hope in the stormy season of those seas, touched at Terceira, where he had the misfortune to lose his brother Paul, companion of his glory, but not destined to share in his triumph.

Leaving Terceira, with its melancholy reminiscences, De Gama, with his battered ships, wrecks of their former selves, containing only one-third of their gallant crews, reached Lisbon in the month of September, 1499.

The reception of De Gama and his companions

by his country, and the honours conferred upon him by his King, present one of those rich pages in the history of the small kingdom of Portugal which the lovers of progress delight to dwell upon; while the benefits conferred on the world by this discovery remain the property of mankind, forming one of the richest contributions towards civilization ever placed on record.

One cannot contemplate, without the most sublime emotion, this spectacle of the conquest of mind over matter. From the first attempt of Don Henry until its fortunate accomplishment in the successful voyage of Vasco de Gama, history cannot record a more glorious triumph than that of the Portuguese discovery of the passage to India. Kings, sages, philosophers, and heroes for the actors; a century for the performance; a vast ocean washing the shores of three continents for the stage; with posterity for the spectators—it stands unparalleled as the great drama of discovery.

It is not our intention, in the present work, to trace the history of Mozambique from its being made known to Europe by the great discovery of

De Gama, through all the changes which have taken place on that coast since the Portuguese era of conquest--nor to show how its position, with that of all the Portuguese settlements in these seas, became affected by the union of Spain and Portugal into one kingdom, and the appearance of the Dutch and English in these seas. These are matters of history, which may be more properly laid before the student of history, the antiquarian, and the lover of social progress, in a work which will shortly appear; while, in a popular work like the present, we will more properly confine ourselves to the state of Mozambique as it may now be seen.

The city of Mozambique is situated on an island of the same name, in latitude 15° 2′ S. and longitude 40° 48′ E., which, with two other islands, St. Jago and St. George, placed in an inlet of the Indian Ocean, form, with the mainland, a secure harbour, five miles deep, and five and a quarter miles broad; and with the neighbouring harbour of Mokambo, in which three rivers discharge themselves, is perhaps the most eligible spot to establish an immense trade with the interior, and an admirable position for an emporium for Europe, America, Arabia, India, and Madagascar. The advantages of this harbour for commercial purposes, both as to its means of communicating with the vast interior of Africa, and the facilities afforded to it by the monsoons for easy access to the neighbouring countries, cannot be overrated. It requires only the entire cessation of the accursed slave-trade to make the capabilities of this magnificent harbour known, when the development of its rich and varied resources would obtain for it a position as an emporium for the commerce of the world, second only to that of Alexandria. As Mohammet Ali restored Alexandria to its former position, so it is in the power of the King ot Portugal, Don Pedro V., to again make Mozambique what it was when first visited by Vasco de Gama, in 1497, namely, a rendezvous for all the commerce of the Indian Ocean. The introduction and fostering of the slave-trade has destroyed legitimate commerce, and reduced it to its present position; and nothing but the entire abolition of that traffic can re-establish its former greatness. The young King of Portugal has a glorious career opened to him, if he will only prove himself worthy of the destiny to which he is called.

On the north end of the island of Mozambique, there is a large fort, called San Sebastian, having an appearance of considerable strength, which at one time no doubt was the case, for it has embrasures for at least eighty pieces of cannon, but barely half of that number are in the fort at present; even the carriages of these are dilapidated by age, and the cannon themselves honey-combed by the combined effects of climate and neglect. This fort would afford but a poor resistance to an attack of one or two small ships of war. But yet the imperial government of Portugal are so intimidated by the occupants of this nest of slavery and piracy, that during my residence at Mozambique, orders were issued that, on the new Governor-general arriving at Mozambique in the month of September, 1857, some of the cannon were to be embarked on board of the frigate which brought him out, for the purpose of being conveyed to Portugal, so as to reduce the strength of the fort, and afford a better chance to the Portuguese government to retake the place, in the event of these slave-dealers attempting to overcome the new Governor-general, and driving him and the local government to obtain safety by flight, as their predecessors had done in 1835.

On the south end of the island there is also a fort, but it is small and of little strength, being intended to command a passage between it and the mainland, which is only practicable for boats, or vessels of very light draught of water.

The city of Mozambique has two churches and three small chapels; the two former were respectable edifices even at the time of their erection, which was when the Portuguese first obtained a footing on this coast. Besides the churches already named, there are one or two fine public buildings. The palace of the Governor-general is a very imposing edifice, of considerable extent, having a court-yard in the middle, from which access is obtained to the reception-rooms, which are lofty, well ventilated, and floored with handsome timber: being an exception to the flooring of all the other houses at Mozambique; the latter being composed of chunam. The palace of the Governor-general was built by the Jesuits for their college, in 1670, but subsequently became, on their expulsion, the property of the government. The roof of it is flat, and entirely covered with lead, which not only protects it against the action of the weather, but renders it cooler than it otherwise would be. It is one of those buildings which strike the eye of the beholder, and give him some idea of the greatness of the Portuguese nation during the era of conquest. The Treasury and the Custom-house are plain, solid buildings, of modern date, and contrast unfavourably with the palace and churches of bygone ages. There is an admirable wharf, which would grace any harbour in Europe, and the masonry of which cannot be surpassed; the portion of it which is under water being built with mortar, in which oil has been used instead of water.

The town is irregularly built, the houses being substantially constructed to resist the heat, and perhaps the earthquakes which are occasionally felt from the volcanic eruptions in the north-west end of Madagascar, and the hurricanes which every five or seven years visit the island with great severity. The streets are very narrow; and the houses being all white-washed, the glare is distressing, and the heat, by these two causes, considerably increased, so that the thermometer is always from six to ten degrees higher in the town than on the mainland. There are two or three squares, and in the principal one there is a pillar of hard wood embedded in masonry, to which the negroes are secured when publicly whipped. Some of the houses have the appearance of comfort, and in former times, when the slave-trade was extensively carried on between Mozambique and Brazil, they were luxuriously furnished, having every comfort which affluence could supply, and the debilitating nature of the climate called for. Since the people of Mozambique have been obliged to abandon slavery, nearly all the former occupants have left, and the remainder, tied to the country by compulsory means, lead a miserable existence engendered by their own vices. The Portuguese officials look with the greatest jealousy upon any of the Mozambique people engaged in the slave-trade, for they consider this traffic as belonging entirely to themselves, and a grant from the government of Portugal, as a compensation in lieu of adequate salaries. There is no mistaking the meaning of the smile and shrug of the shoulders with which they reply to any one who ventures to state that the Portuguese government is sincere in its endeavour to suppress the slave-trade. I have been told, by persons in Mozambique, "Yes, the government of Portugal, after ruining us, are sincere in their endeavours to prevent us engaging in the traffic; and they take the best mode to prevent us benefiting by that traffic, for they send out their officers here on paltry salaries, which they well know cannot support life, and make them prevent us engaging in the slave-trade. But the government of the King knows well that the soldiers have not been paid for more than four years, and that many of the officers have not received a *vintim*, or farthing, from the treasury, for more than two years. How must these men live? By the slave-trade. So that they deprive us of the benefits which were formerly derived from the slave-trade; and to prevent legal commerce, which would supplant the trade in the natives, they throw every obstacle in our way."

I must say, I observed, while at Mozambique, that this was a very fair statement of the case.

The city of Mozambique is exceedingly dirty, from the filthy habits of the Portuguese; and, without going into particulars, it may be briefly stated that it is the filthiest city in the universe, not even excepting that of Lisbon. For which there is not the shadow of an excuse, as there is an overabundance of slaves without employment; and the town being built on the beach, where the tide has a rise and a fall of, at times, twelve feet, there can be no difficulty in keeping it clean. That indolence which to the modern Portuguese has now become proverbially natural, has here an opportunity for its fullest development, so that the air they breathe, both here and in all the settlements along the coast, is as foul as the immorality in which they live.

The inhabitants of Mozambique are about 7,000 in number. The garrison, consisting of Portuguese soldiers, in all under 200, are principally convicts;

some portion of them being convicts who have already passed a term of penal servitude at Goâ, and are sent from that place to serve a further period of punishment at Mozambique for crimes committed at the former settlement.

There are a few Portuguese officials connected with the Custom-house and the Treasury, some half-caste descendants of Portuguese or Canarines from Goâ, and natural children of slave-dealers by native women from India or Africa; such is the society at Mozambique. Add to this, one German merchant and an agent of a house from Marseilles, thirty or forty Banyan traders from Cutch, Goâ, and Bombay; a few Arabs, or, as they are called at Mozambique, Moors, and you have all that portion of the inhabitants of the island who call themselves free. The remaining portion of the inhabitants are slaves, called Négros, or, by the Christian Portuguese, they are more generally styled *Gentiles*.

The aspect of the town from the anchorage is that of former grandeur crumbling to decay; and, indeed, a more intimate acquaintance realized the impression made on first entering the harbour.

There are generally a few vessels, principally Portuguese, lying in the harbour; and in the healthy season, which is also the trading season here, a great number of dhows from different places on the west coast of India, the Persian Gulf, Red Sea, Madagascar, Comoro Islands, Zanzibar, and along the whole east coast of Africa, are attracted here, in the face of Portuguese restrictions on trade, by the enormous profits to be derived by trading at this place. If the slave-trade was done away with once and for ever, legitimate traffic with the whole Indian Ocean and adjoining seas might be indefinitely developed, and realize to Portugal a princely revenue. This might be done by simply removing those persons from Mozambique who are well known to the Portuguese government as being engaged in the slave-trade, and without whose assistance the Portuguese officials, arriving at Mozambique strangers to the country, could not engage in selling the natives. The names of these slave-dealers have been communicated to the Portuguese government, and it is nothing but the influence which they maintain, by bribing largely parties who have access to the ministers, and others who are all-powerful at the Court of Lisbon, which prevents the government of the King from taking so simple a course; viz., the banishment of a few individuals for the benefit of the community. It will be asserted, on the other hand, that this would be a dangerous step to take, as these well-known persons have great influence at Mozambique, where their long residence has given them great influence over the natives, and where they form a local party, which, aided by the climate, the poverty of the Portuguese government, and the treachery of the officials and officers, renders them all-powerful. To this I simply reply, that the Portuguese government, to my certain knowledge, holds in its possession undisputed proofs of the guilt of these slave-dealers; and it is only by a guilty connivance of some members of the government of the King, who are participators in their ill-gotten and infamous gains, that measures have not been taken ere this for preventing, by banishment of those engaged in this traffic at Mozambique, a crime revolting to humanity, and opposed to Christianity and civilization.

The statements made in this narrative of facts, which came to my knowledge while at Mozambique, and which are so notorious that the government of Portugal offers no denial to them, fully justify the charges of complicity made against the government of the King, and show that the efforts made by that government are a continued imposition on the credulity of England and other nations engaged in this great question of the cause of humanity.

The remedy is simple, while the proof of sincerity on the part of Portugal in suppressing the odious traffic is very easy.

Banish those persons who are well known to be engaged in the slave-trade, change *all* the officials, and encourage the emigration of 1000 Europeans to the province of Mozambique, that territory would soon be richer than the Brazils, and many of the Brazilian planters would invest in land, and develop the resources of a country where labour is so plentiful that the sugar-growing countries have obtained their labour from it for ages.

But to do this effectually it will be necessary, and only just, to give to the officials going out to be employed under the new system salaries adequate to their wants. Pay them well and make them honest. Now they obtain an appointment at Mozambique, with a salary which is not sufficient for their requirements even in Portugal. How insufficient must it be for their wants in a country where everything European in manufacture is naturally increased in price, and where the climate renders many of those things looked upon as luxuries in Europe absolutely necessary for the support of the European constitution. At present, when a Portuguese official is appointed to a post at Mozambique, his salary is an uncertain small amount, frequently not paid from one to four years after it has become due; but the appointment is known to be worth so much more, because those who have held it have returned to Portugal with a certain amount of wealth, that amount well known to the government and nation at large; and also as well known the means by which that wealth was obtained; namely, the buying and selling the great product of the country which has alone been developed—that of its natives.

These human beings are bought from their relations or their enemies, and are supplied to the slave ship at an enormous profit. A Portuguese official knows the terms on which he takes the appointment—a small salary and the opportunity of making a large fortune by the slave-trade. These appointments are consequently eagerly sought after; and the cadets of noble families in Portugal are indeed deemed fortunate who obtain them. Is it then a wonder, when they arrive at Mozambique, that they use all possible means to amass wealth by the slave-trade, and look upon the Portarias of the King of Portugal as a sham before the world, and an infringement of the rights vested in them by the appointment which they may hold from the King?

From this it will be seen that the fault entirely rests with the government of Portugal, and that by paying the officials properly honesty will be secured. At present a premium is conferred on slave-dealers; for those who are most successful in amassing wealth by the nefarious traffic obtain, on reaching Portugal, by means of that wealth, titles, honours (?), and consideration,—year after year adding to the degradation which has come on Portugal through the slave-trade, and the slave-trade alone.

CHAPTER XV.

Slave-Trade under the French Flag—Vessels Employed—How Fitted and Provisioned—Price Paid for Slaves by the French—Ceremony of Engaging the "Labourers"—How Treated at Réunion—Dhows Employed, and Horrors of the Traffic—Statement of the Captain of a French Trading Vessel—Statement of the Supercargo of an American Trading Vessel—Revolt of Slaves on Board of a French Brig, and Massacre of the Crew—How the Slaves are obtained in the Interior of Africa—The Natives Rise *en masse*—Feelings of the Natives towards British Consul and Family—The "Zambesi" assisting the "Minnetonka" to obtain Slaves.

SOON after my arrival at Mozambique, I determined to make myself thoroughly master of the details of the slave-trade carried on from this Portuguese province, by vessels under the French flag, to the French colony of Réunion or Bourbon. The following is the result of my inquiries on the subject. I will first state how the traffic is carried on, and in what manner the slaves are treated at Réunion; and then enter fully into the particulars of obtaining the slaves in the interior of Africa for the supply of this traffic; showing to what serious results these operations in the interior led under my own observation at Mozambique.

The vessels employed in the FRENCH SLAVE TRADE, from the east coast of Africa to the island of Réunion, are vessels sailing under the French flag, from 200 to 1000 tons burthen; one screw steamer, the "Mascareinnes," has also been employed.

These vessels all start from the island of Réunion, and to legalize this traffic in slaves a French agent of the Governor of Bourbon is placed on board each vessel. These agents, at first, were French military officers, but the commandant of the troops at that island found that this traffic was so demoralizing to the officers, that he could not of late be prevailed upon to allow his subordinates to be employed in the capacity of slave-dealers, and for these officers, clerks in the French commodore's office at Réunion were substituted.

These slave-dealers employed as agents of the Governor of Réunion, to give to them some appearance of respectability, are designated FRENCH DELEGATES; and the slave-trade, which they are employed in is styled THE FRENCH FREE LABOUR EMIGRATION TRADE.

Each vessel employed in this trade is allowed to carry one negro per ton burthen; but, in the case of some ships that can carry more than their registered tonnage, an increase is allowed, being as high sometimes as 30 per cent.

Most of the large vessels are fitted with an apparatus for distilling water.

Before leaving Réunion, the ships are visited by the authorities appointed for that purpose; and the DELEGATE embarks to witness the legality and voluntary nature of the agreement made with the negroes.

The rations allowed to the negroes are ample; they consist of rice and salt fish, and a liberal allowance of water.

IBO, a Portuguese possession, the principal

of the Querimba Islands, off Cape Delgado, is the general rendezvous for those vessels which proceed direct to the east coast of Africa.

The price paid for the negroes is from 30 to 40 dollars per head, from 12 to 18 dollars of the purchase-money, in each case, being divided between the Governor-general of the province of Mozambique, the Procureur du Roi, the Juge de Droit, and the Governors of Ibo, Killimane, or any other Portuguese possession where the embarkation takes place.

The slaves, for the supply of this traffic, are kept generally at a distance of two or three days' journey from the coast, on account of the scarcity of food; and also that the barracoons, in which they are imprisoned until required for exportation, may not be seen by the British ships of war employed on the coast for the suppression of the slave-trade.

These slaves are brought from the INTERIOR, and are sometimes two, three, and even four months on their journey to the barracoons.

There can be no doubt that they are obtained by violence.

On reaching the deck of the French ship, the ceremony of engaging the slaves as Free Labourers is gone through by an Arab interpreter, who asks them, in the presence of the DELEGATE, whether they voluntarily engage to serve for five years at Réunion. The interpreter assures the DELEGATE that the slave is willing to become a Free Labourer at Réunion, in every instance. The DELEGATE cannot speak the native language, and does not know what question the slave is asked, nor the nature of his reply, but being assured by the Arab that the slave is willing to go to Réunion, the FRENCH DELEGATE is satisfied, and if asked if the slaves are willing to leave Africa, he declares, on *his honour*, that " he does not know anything to the contrary." This is a true and simple statement of the manner in which the slave is engaged.

Once on board the French Free Labour Emigration ships, the slaves are generally treated with humanity, and are well fed; it being, of course, the interest of the captains of the vessels engaged in this traffic to land their cargoes in good condition.

Occasionally, from mismanagement, neglect, or inhumanity, the slaves become irritated and rebel; and if they have the good fortune to overcome their oppressors, the wrongs which they have suffered are avenged by a general massacre of the Europeans on board.

Upon the arrival of the vessels at Réunion, the SLAVES, now called FREE LABOURERS, are immediately vaccinated, and the sick placed in hospital, at the expense of the captain or importer. Those who are in good health, after passing fourteen days' quarantine, in buildings devoted to that purpose, are hired to different sugar planters for a term of five years. These planters pay to the importer the expense of importing the FREE LABOURER, or, in other words, the market value of the SLAVE.

The negroes have no choice of masters. They receive as wages from six to eight shillings per month, and their food, which consists of rice, salt fish, and salt; in addition to which the employer has to find them clothes, and medical attendance when sick.

In each district there is an officer styled PROTECTOR OF IMMIGRANTS, whose business it is to see that these men are not ill-used, and that they receive in *cash*, at the end of every month, the wages that may be due to them.

On no pretence is the employer allowed to strike his African Free Labourer; if the man behaves ill, he will be punished by the proper authorities.

Each immigrant is provided with a book, in which his name is inscribed, together with that of his employer, and the rate of wages which the free labourer is to receive.

At the end of each month, the planter must appear with his labourer before the Protector of Immigrants, in whose presence the wages are paid, and the signature of the Protector of Immigrants in the immigrant's book is a receipt for the free labourer's wages.

Should the master neglect this, and pay the labourer at his own house, or out of the presence of the Protector of Immigrants, the transaction is illegal, and he can be compelled to pay the wages a second time. I have heard of a case in point, where a free labourer had been receiving his wages for more than two years, without being paid in the presence of the Protector of Immigrants. He was induced to demand the wages to be paid over again for that period, and, I am told, the law was enforced.

At the end of five years the negro must be returned to his own country, at the expense of the original importer; but this very rarely happens, excepting in the case of the Malagasy, who are obtained in St. Augustine Bay, at the south-west end of Madagascar. Those who elect to remain in Réunion generally take service by the month, and obtain wages from fourteen to sixteen shillings per month and their food. Mechanics, such as carpenters, masons, and blacksmiths, receive higher wages.

Some of the French vessels engaged in this traffic proceed to Nossi-bé, the French settlement off the north-west end of Madagascar, and put themselves in communication with the Arab merchants or Antealoats, in Majunga Bay. An Arab belonging to Zanzibar, named Kallifan, is generally employed.

The vessel remains anchored at Nossi-bé whilst

the Arabs send their dhows to the coast of Africa to obtain the slaves who are landed on a given point on the coast of Madagascar.

These dhows are from twenty to fifty tons burthen, generally without decks, and as the Arabs know well that they are liable to be seized, even when empty, by the British ships of war engaged in the suppression of the slave-trade, if they have mats, provisions, or any extra cooking apparatus on board, they take nothing more than what is absolutely necessary for their own crews. No provision is made for the comfort of the expected living cargo.

The slaves forming the cargoes of these dhows are obtained by purchase or by theft—to the Arab it is a matter of indifference how he obtains them—by purchase, by fraud, or by force. When the cargo is complete, the slaves are tied hand and foot, and then placed on board the dhow.

During the voyage to the rendezvous they receive just sufficient *uncooked* rice or beans, with a little water, to keep them alive, and are left, day and night, without any covering whatever, bound hand and foot, not being even released to attend to the calls of nature. The interior of the dhow therefore becomes a putrid mass of living corruption; numbers of the slaves dying from fever, dysentery, and small-pox, engendered by the pestilential atmosphere within the hold of the slave dhow.

Their destination is generally some port not likely to be visited by Her Majesty's cruisers; and, arrived there, the only improvement in their condition is a full allowance of water. Should it happen that by stress of weather, or any other cause, the French ship that is to take them is retarded in her arrival, their sufferings are much increased; and when these poor creatures do at last get on board the French ship, the sudden change to an ample diet produces sickness, and sometimes death.

The captain of a French trading vessel stated that, on one occasion when he landed at Europa Island, at the southern end of the Mozambique Channel, to obtain some turtle, he found upwards of a hundred negroes lying on the beach, without any protection against the sun, wind, or rain;

they were guarded by some armed Arabs, and were waiting the arrival of a vessel to take them to Réunion. Their provisions were nearly exhausted; and if by any accident the vessel whose cargo they were intended to form should be retarded in her arrival at Europa Island, it is easy to conceive what their fate would be.

As the Arab dhows employed on this service are, for the most part, old and unseaworthy, and they often lose their way, there can be no doubt that numbers of negroes on board die from starvation.

The supercargo of an American vessel which I visited in Mozambique harbour, in the month of February, 1858, told me that on his leaving Nossi-bé, a week previous to my seeing him, there were four French vessels waiting there for cargoes of free labourers; and that, during his stay at that port, news arrived that the price of free labourers had fallen to one hundred dollars at Réunion, where it had been gradually decreasing since the month of September, 1857, in consequence of the market becoming overstocked. He said that there was no difference between free labourers and slaves, as carried on at Nos-si-bé; for that on board of free labour ships the slaves had all heavy logs of hard wood securing both ancles; and that, if they wanted to move from one place to another, they had to carry the log to enable them to do so.

He stated his opinion that, if Great Britain permitted France to carry on the SLAVE-TRADE under the denomination of FREE LABOUR, vessels would soon be found in the Mozambique Channel from the Southern States of America, under the American flag, and with an American Delegate on board, authorized to purchase slaves, and call them American Free Labourers.

He had heard that the slaves on board two of the so-called French Free Labour ships had risen and destroyed all the French on board.

I subsequently learned that the circumstances attending the destruction of the French on board one of these vessels were truly revolting. It appears that the vessel, a small French brig, was at anchor in one of the harbours at the north-west end of Madagascar; she had completed her cargo, and was on the eve of departure. The captain had gone on shore to settle matters with the Arab procurer, and the mate and crew were preparing for weighing the anchor. In an instant, without any warning, a cry was heard among the oppressed. The slaves had risen, and a fierce struggle took place between the oppressor and the oppressed, in which the latter were victorious. With the exception of one man, who saved himself by jumping overboard, the French were cruelly murdered, the slaves wreaking their vengeance even on the inanimate forms of the dead, which they subjected to the most revolting indignities long after life was extinct. The captain's son, a mere youth, the slaves put to the most excruciating torments, under which he perished.

They cut the head off the dead body, and placed it on the figure-head of the vessel. They gutted the vessel, set her on fire, and then escaped to the shore. With these facts before us, with which the French government are well acquainted, I ask whether the slaves obtained for the French Free Labour, from the north-west end of Madagascar, are free agents?

It will now be my duty to state how the SLAVES

are obtained in Mozambique, for the supply of the FRENCH SLAVE-TRADE TO RÉUNION.

When this description of traffic in human beings was renewed at Mozambique, under the new denomination of French Free Labour Emigration, there was a surplus of slaves in all the Portuguese settlements on the east coast of Africa; and the Governor-general of Mozambique, and his subordinates, found no difficulty in supplying the demand for the first twelve months, that is to say, from 1854 to 1855; for the Portuguese residents were only too glad to sell to the Portuguese officials those slaves whom the orders of the government of Portugal had prevented being supplied to the regular slave ships from Cuba, and the southern ports of the United States; and the effect of this trade was to rid Mozambique of a great portion of its slave population, with which it was overburdened. After the first twelve months of the traffic, slaves became scarce, the price rose, the demand still increased, but the French slave-dealers were unwilling to give the prices now demanded by the residents in Mozambique. To supply the demand, keep prices low, and secure the enormous profits which the Governor-general of Mozambique, and his partners in this nefarious traffic, were enjoying, it became necessary to send into the interior for slaves. At first, it was found that the chiefs in the interior refused to comply with the demands of the Moors or Arabs, who went there for the purchase of slaves, alleging as a reason that it was contrary to the wishes of the Portuguese government that there should be any more traffic in slaves; and the Moors, on their return to Mozambique, declared to the Governor-general that they could not, in consequence, supply the demand.

To prove to the chiefs in the interior that the Moors went with the consent of the Portuguese authorities in search of slaves for the French Free Labour Emigration, some of the Portuguese soldiers, who had been living with the women of the country, and had acquired the Makua language, were despatched with the Moors into the interior, and the uniforms of the soldiers of the King of Portugal were found a sufficient guarantee to the chiefs in the interior that the slave-trade was authorized by the Portuguese government, and immediately they set to work to supply the traffic in earnest; by these means the prices of slaves were kept low at Mozambique, the Portuguese officials made enormous gains, and the French Free Labour Emigration flourished. Meanwhile, all the horrors which had accompanied the slave-trade in the interior of Africa in former times were revived. Parents sold their children, and every available slave was disposed of to supply the demand; but, this increasing, recourse was had to arms, for the purpose of capturing individual prisoners. Numbers perished in the deadliest warfare. This state of things was brought about by the Moors and the Portuguese soldiers, who had accompanied them to procure the slaves. I have, myself, conversed with some of the actors in these scenes, and the facts which I have stated cannot be denied.

At last a reaction took place; the natives found that they were destroying each other to obtain a few prisoners for the supply of the slave-trade which the Portuguese were carrying on; and, for a time, they ceased from warfare, and again there was a scarcity in the slave market at Mozambique.

During the two years which had elapsed since the commencement of this traffic, attention had been drawn to the facility with which slaves were obtained on the east coast of Africa, and the slave-dealers at Cuba turned their attention to Mozambique. We shall presently see them competing with the French in their slavery operations on the east coast of Africa.

The new demand on the slave market in Mozambique, caused by the arrival of Spanish and American slavers, induced the Governor-general of Mozambique to again despatch the soldiers of his king to the interior, in order to assist the Moors in their operations. At first they were again successful; but, at last, the Negroes, exasperated by the bloodshed which had again commenced among them, and attributing it to its correct cause, viz., the presence of the Portuguese soldiers among them, rose and destroyed some of them, and the survivors escaped only with their lives, to bring to the city of Mozambique the intelligence that all the natives had risen with the intention of driving the Portuguese into the sea. This was found no idle threat, for the detachment of soldiers stationed at the Palace of Messuril, on the mainland of Cabaceira, situated at about five miles distance from my house, was attacked about a month after my arrival at Mozambique. All the troops, with the exception of a sergeant and eight invalids, were removed from the city of Mozambique (which, being on an island, was considered secure), and encamped round the village of Messuril. For three weeks the Portuguese troops were in hourly expectation of an attack, and it was only in consequence of the great influence which one Portuguese had over the natives that they were prevented from annihilating the Portuguese troops. It appears that this officer, who had resided at Mozambique for more than fifty years, had quarrelled with the Governor-general of Mozambique, in consequence of being deprived of what he considered his just share of the head money obtained by the Portuguese officials from the French Free Labour Emigration. And when matters at Messuril had arrived at a crisis, he was induced by the inhabitants of the city to arrange his differences with the Governor-general, and save the Portuguese dominion in this part of the world. He did so, went among the natives, and, in three days' time, by bribes and creating mutual jealousies among the native chiefs, he induced them to abandon their intentions, but with the stipulation that no more attempts would be made to obtain slaves from their country.

During the time this was going on at Messuril, to show the feelings of the natives towards myself, I ought to state that my wife, accompanied by her maid, drove through numbers of these natives unmolested. They knew well who the British Consul was, and the purpose for which I was sent to Mozambique; and they hailed my presence among them on all occasions with the liveliest satisfaction, frequently presenting my wife with flowers and fruit.

On the day of the threatened attack, previous to the intervention of the old Brigadier, numbers of slaves came into the compound of my house, bringing their native beds and cooking utensils, and pointing to the British consular flag flying over my house, assured me that they would be safe with me, if I would only allow them to remain; for the natives had determined only to spare my house and those within it. A sickly Portuguese soldier, who was lent to me as an interpreter, stated that even he would be safe with me. While this was going on, I sent a messenger to my neighbour, the Brigadier Soares, who was looked upon as the Metternich of Mozambique, and he sent me back word to say that he was ready to receive the natives, for he had 200 armed negroes in the gateway of his house, and at the same time stated that I had nothing to fear, for the natives knew very well who I was.

Similarly, Salt, who visited Mozambique in 1809, tells us that—

"The Makuas are a strong, athletic race of people, very formidable, and constantly in the habit of making incursions into the small tract of territory which the Portuguese possess on the coast. Their enmity is inveterate, and is confessed to have arisen from the shameful practices of the traders, who have gone among them to purchase slaves. They fight chiefly with spears, darts, and poisoned arrows; but they also possess no inconsiderable number of muskets, which they procure in the northern districts from the Arabs, and very frequently, as the governor assured me, from the Portuguese dealers themselves, who, in the eager pursuit of wealth, are thus content to barter their own security for gold, slaves, and ivory, which they get in return.

"These obnoxious neighbours have latterly been quiet, but in their last incursion they advanced with such a force into the peninsula of Cabaceira, as actually to oblige the Portuguese to quit the field. In their progress they destroyed the plantations, burnt the slave-huts, and killed or carried off every person who fell into their hands. They penetrated even into the fort of Messuril, and threw down the image of St. John, which was in the chapel, plundering the one adjoining the Government House, and converted the priest's dress, in which he celebrates mass, into a habit of ceremony for their chief. This occurred about three years ago, and most clearly evinces the very weak and precarious state of the settlement."—(*A Voyage to Abyssinia, &c., by Henry Salt, F.R.S., London,* 1814, *p.* 38.)

Salt also quotes Purchas, who mentions a similar incursion of the Makuas, in 1585, for which see Purchas, vol. ii., p. 1553.

On my arrival at Mozambique, I had carefully searched the official bulletin to see if the order of the Portuguese government, and the Portarias of the King of Portugal, dated 27th February, 1855, and 30th July, 1856, forbidding any participation in the French Free Labour traffic, had been published for the information of all parties. Finding it had not been published, and that consequently any one engaged in supplying slaves for that traffic might state in his justification that the traffic was established in Mozambique under the authority of the Governor-general of Mozambique, and consequently sanctioned by the Portuguese government, I considered it only proper to ask the Governor-general whether he had received the Portarias referred to. He said he had not, and expressed his astonishment that they had not been furnished to him. I immediately offered to furnish him with a copy of these Portarias, under my hand and seal, when he applied to the secretary of the government for information on the subject, and he was reminded by that functionary that he had received them some time previously. I urged upon him the necessity of giving them publicity; he acknowledged the good it might do, and stated that he would have them published immediately. A reference to the official bulletin will show that they were not published until after the arrival of his successor.

I soon discovered that the French Free Labour Emigration, and the Spanish and American Slave-Trade, were carried on by the Governor-general, and nearly all the officials in the Portuguese settlements on the east coast of Africa, and that the residents at those places (with the exception of the most influential, who could assist the traffic) were not allowed to interfere in it; and, if found doing so, were punished. We now come to proofs of my statements.

I have already, in the course of this personal narrative, referred to the "Minnetonka" barque, under American colours, as having called off the Port of Natal, in the month of June, 1857, and of the exertions made by H.M.S. "Hermes," which conveyed myself and family to Mozambique, to capture that vessel.

In the month of March, 1857, the British barque "Ocean Queen" ran on shore, and became a total wreck on the Bazarutto Islands, in the Mozambique Channel. Some portion of the crew reached the small Portuguese village on one of those islands, and for five months were hospitably entertained by the Governor of the island, who, on being informed by the shipwrecked sailors that they had nothing with which to reward him, nobly replied, "God will reward me." This conduct of the Governor of the Bazarutto Islands having come to my knowledge, and not having been called upon to re-imburse him for the support of five of my countrymen for the period of five months, it became my pleasing duty to bring this generous conduct under the notice of the British government, and to urge upon it the propriety of making some suitable acknowledgment; and I have much pleasure in stating that my application in favour of the Portuguese Governor has been generously responded to by Her Majesty's government.

The Portuguese schooner-of-war, "Zambesi," arrived at the Bazarutto Islands early in June; and the shipwrecked party of mariners belonging to the late barque "Ocean Queen," so long and hospitably entertained by the Portuguese Governor, were ordered a passage on board the schooner, for the purpose of being conveyed to Mozambique, and placed under the protection of Her Majesty's Consul there. The "Zambesi" had on board, as a passenger, Major Olliveira, who was sent to supersede the then Governor of Inhambane, a naval officer, the Capitain de Corvette Leotti, in consequence of the latter refusing to give to the Governor-general of Mozambique the six dollars per head which he claimed as his share of head-money for every slave leaving Inhambane, either on board of a FRENCH FREE LABOUR EMIGRATION SHIP, or any other SLAVER.

The "Zambesi" proceeded to Inhambane, Major Olliveira relieved Capitain de Corvette Leotti, and, in about three weeks' time, the "Zambesi" prepared to return to the Bazarutto Islands and Mozambique.

The evening before she crossed the bar of the Inhambane river, a barque was observed to stand in from sea, and anchor off Barrow Hill; this was the American barque "Minnetonka," under American colours, commanded by Captain Ward, and belonging to the Brothers Cabargas at the Havannah; the same vessel which called off Port Natal on the 22nd of June, just a week previous, to inquire if she could obtain a cargo of slaves at that British colony. There she was unsuccessful, and was obliged to fly from the dreaded British cruiser; but here, in a Portuguese colony, with a Portuguese man-of-war alongside of her, she had nothing to fear.

On the next morning the "Zambesi" got under weigh; and, as soon as she had crossed the bar of the river, she shaped a course for the Spanish slaver under American colours, not to capture, but to assist her. The American captain, knowing well the people he had to deal with, lowered a boat, and sent his boatswain in her to communicate with the captain of the Portuguese vessel-of-war, and ask his advice as to the best mode of obtaining a cargo of slaves.

On board the "Zambesi" was the Capitain de Corvette Leotti, late Governor of Inhambane, who had been superseded for defying the Governor-general of Mozambique, and refusing to give him his share of slave head-money. Leotti was a buccaneer in heart, although he wore the uniform of the King of Portugal. He had lost his governorship, and now obtained an opportunity of making a fortune. The "Minnetonka" had 70,000 dollars on board, all of which the American captain would give in exchange for slaves; and he would be back in a time agreed upon for the cargo. Matters were arranged at once; the boatswain was desired to accompany to the shore the pilot of the "Zambesi," the King of Portugal's pilot, it is true, but, nevertheless, a pilot ready to assist a slaver at all times. Leotti sent instructions to his agents on shore, and hoisted a flag, as a signal to the American captain, that his instructions would be complied with, and the slaves ready at the time he wished.

The "Minnetonka" stood to sea to avoid any British cruiser which might be hovering off the coast. Fear not, "Minnetonka," the

Mozambique Channel is clear of British cruisers, and the senior naval officer has reported that "he has reason to believe no slaver has been fitted on the east coast, or taken away slaves round the Cape of Good Hope for the last three years." * There is one man upon your track who judges for himself, and does not take slave-dealers' reports; but he has not yet entered the Mozambique Channel; he is at Natal, and has only just heard of your movements. You may perhaps obtain your cargo of slaves, and add to the large list of unreported slavers which have been carrying large cargoes from the Mozambique to Cuba and America for a quarter of a century.

The "Zambesi" stood away for the Bazarutto Islands, remained there three days, relanded the men who had belonged to the "Ocean Queen," and returned to Inhambane. It would not answer that the Englishmen should witness what was about to be enacted at Inhambane, and therefore they were left at the Bazarutto Islands.

On the return of Leotti to Inhambane, he en-

* See Anti-Slavery Reporter (Supplement), July 1, 1859, p. 2.

deavoured to obtain possession of the government of that place, but Major Olliveira was too strong for him, and he did not succeed. His object in attempting this rebellious act was to obtain the profit which he would derive from supplying the "Minnetonka" with a cargo of slaves.

At the appointed time the "Minnetonka" called at Inhambane, but as they had only at that time 200 slaves to supply her with, she proceeded to the northward, and soon afterwards ran into the anchorage at Ibo. Here she found seven of the French Free Labour Emigration vessels waiting anxiously for their cargoes. The price of slaves at Ibo, for the supply of the French Free Labour Emigration when the "Minnetonka" went into Ibo, was 40 dollars per head. The Governor of Ibo supplied the captain of the "Minnetonka" with 1200 slaves at 70 dollars per head. These slaves had been obtained for the French Free Labour Emigration ships, but were supplied to the "Minnetonka" because the captain of that vessel gave a higher price than the captains of the French slavers. And from that fact alone the destination of these 1200 souls was changed from Réunion to Cuba—from the tri-colour of France to that of Spain.

The captains of the French slavers waited on the Governor of Ibo, and remonstrated with him on the injustice of re-selling the slaves obtained for them to the Spanish slaver under American colours, but obtained no redress.

Subsequently a Spanish barque called the "Venus" arrived at Ibo, and also a Spanish brig, both vessels requiring slaves for Cuba. The Governor of Ibo was going to supply them; but the captains of the French slavers waited upon the Portuguese Governor, and would not permit him to supply those vessels. They also informed the captains of the Spanish slavers that if they did not immediately proceed to sea they would set their vessels on fire.

The brig went to Inhambane, and obtained the slaves which had been collected for the "Minnetonka." She was afterwards chased by H.M.S. "Geyser," which vessel lost sight of her in a heavy squall, and gave up the chase. The brig, one hour after the chase had been given up by the "Geyser," lost her fore-topmast, and would of course have been an easy and certain prize had the "Geyser" continued the chase a little longer.

The barque "Venus" ran into the anchorage at Zanzibar under Spanish colours, and anchored between H.M.S.V. "Hermes" and a French ship-of-war lying there. She obtained a clearance to ship a cargo of hides at Lamu, a town belonging to the Imâm of Muskat, in 2° south latitude, and from that place went away with a cargo of 800 slaves. The young Imâm of Muskat sent for the Governor of Lamu to give an explanation of this affair, with which he appeared satisfied, for he returned him to his Governorship at Lamu in one of his ships of war.

On my calling the attention of the Governor-general of Mozambique to the slave-trade as carried on at Ibo, he stated that he could not interfere by superseding the Governor of Ibo, because, although subordinate to himself, he was appointed by the King. The fact was that the Governor of Ibo kept his accounts properly; that is to say, he gave the Governor-general of Mozambique six dollars for every slave who left Ibo, and therefore he would not supersede him as he had done Leotti.

On the arrival of the new Governor-general, the Governor of Ibo was immediately superseded, on my calling attention to my dispatches addressed to his Excellency's predecessor relative to slaving there. On the other hand, the Governor of Ibo sent down, in an open boat, by a relation of the Governor-general who kept him in office, only a few nights before the new Governor-general arrived, 12,000 dollars, as his superior's share of head-money. So that we may believe that there is even honour among slave-dealers.

Some of the other officials did not treat Vasco Guedes so well. As soon as they heard he was to be superseded, they behaved like Leotti, and wished to treat the Judge in the same way; but he went down to Killimane and other places along the coast, and by threatening the Governors with the utmost rigour of the law, he obtained from them his share, viz.—three dollars per head for every slave exported under any denomination.

The facts above stated may be easily obtained

by a reference to the last Slave-trade Papers laid before Parliament, and are confirmed by documents in the possession of the British, Portuguese, and French governments. I state facts, without divulging any secrets, and I defy the Portuguese to disprove them. Inquiry will only elicit other circumstances which ought to be made public. As it may not be convenient for the reader to refer to the documents which have been laid before Parliament, I will here produce the evidence of the Portuguese ship of war "Zambesi" assisting the "Minnetonka" in obtaining slaves.

Extract from the deposition of Henry Batt, second mate of the late barque "Ocean Queen," wrecked on the Bazarutto Islands, on the 3rd March, 1857:—*

"On or about the 1st June, the Portuguese schooner of war, 'Zambesi,' arrived at Santa Carolina with dispatches for the Governor of the Bazarutto Islands. She had on board, as a passenger, Major Olliveira, the new Governor of In-

* *Vide* Slave-trade Papers, laid before both Houses of Parliament, 1858-9.

hambane, sent by the Governor-general of Mozambique to supersede the Governor Leotti. She left Santa Carolina on the 5th June, and in her myself, and the crew of the 'Ocean Queen,' were sent to Inhambane. About the 12th June we arrived at Inhambane, and remained there about three weeks.

"The 'Zambesi' returning to Bazarutto, we were ordered to go in her.

"29th June, weighed and stood for the bar; anchored in ten fathoms, abreast of Mafouroon Island. About ten, A.M., on the 30th of June, still at anchor; observed a clipper barque, painted all black, standing in for Barrow Hill; she stood off and on there till she clewed up everything and anchored off there about three P.M. The same afternoon the pilot came on board the 'Zambesi;' blowing strong from the S.W.

"Next morning weighed, and proceeded; after crossing the bar stood to the southward, and observed a boat lowered from the barque at anchor off Barrow Hill. This boat, with the boatswain of the barque and four men, came alongside of the 'Zambesi;' after she had been alongside about five minutes, and the boatswain of the barque had conversed during that time with the captain of the 'Zambesi' and the late Governor Leotti, of Inhambane, as a signal to the barque, a white flag was hoisted at the fore-top-gallant mast-head, and a similar one at the peak.

"The 'Zambesi' now stood for the barque, which immediately made sail, slipped from her anchor, and stood out to sea. The pilot, in his own boat, accompanied the boat of the barque to Inhambane, and we in the schooner proceeded to the Bazarutto Islands.

"During the time that the boat of the barque was alongside the 'Zambesi,' I had a conversation with one of the men belonging to the boat, who spoke English. He informed me that some time previous they anchored on the coast, further to the south, where the mate and an armed boat's crew went on shore to obtain slaves; he believed that this party had been murdered by the natives. Observing a vessel to the southward, which they believed to be an English man-of-war, they slipped, and ran away to the northward and eastward, towards Madagascar, from which island they came to Inhambane. In reply to a question, he said, with a laugh, that he had quite forgotten the name of the barque, but that she was under American colours; the crew were principally Spaniards; they had plenty of powder on board; they were well armed, and could show fight; they had six guns, and were well armed for boarders; they had irons down below for the negroes when they got them on board, and a large stock of provisions, and a great deal of money for purchasing slaves. He had heard the captain of the barque say that he thought he would be able to get the slaves at Inhambane.

"When the barque made sail, the man with whom I had been conversing spoke to the boatswain about it, and he replied, 'That is nothing, she will be back in a few days.'

"Eight days after this, we arrived at Santa Carolina, where we were landed. The 'Zambesi' remained at Santa Carolina two or three days, and then returned to Mozambique with the late Governor Leotti. I wished to go to Inhambane in the 'Zambesi,' but I was not allowed to do so.

"In about a month's time, the 'Zambesi' with Leotti on board, returned to Santa Carolina; she remained there two days, and then we and Leotti came up in her to Mozambique.

"(Signed) HENRY BATT,
"*Second Mate.*

"*Witness to Signature.*
"(Signed) JOHN TURNER."

On bringing these circumstances under the notice of the Governor-general of Mozambique, he admitted the correctness of all the statements made by me relative to the "Zambesi" communicating with the "Minnetonka," and stated that he had delivered both the Commander of the "Zambesi," and the Ex-governor Leotti to the proper tribunals. To this I replied that I was aware that the Moor, who happened to be in command of the "Zambesi," had been imprisoned; but that I was also aware that the Ex-governor Leotti, under whose orders the Moor acted, was still at large. He then stated that he had taken his sword from Leotti, and forbade his leaving the island of Mozambique, and that he had now released the Moor from prison, placing both of them in the same condition.

The Moor, I learned, had been kept in command of the "Zambesi," because the officer who ought properly to have commanded that ship refused to do the bidding of the Governor-general of Mozambique, in communicating with slavers, and seizing legal traders. This fact is well known, not only in Mozambique, but also at Lisbon; but the deserving officer who would not prostitute himself, his uniform, and the "Zambesi" to the nefarious practices of Vasco Guedes, will go unrewarded. It is by losing these opportunities of promoting the deserving that the Portuguese government have established the reputation of neglecting merit and advancing knaves.

Eight months after this action had occurred, and after numerous failures to collect the members of the Court, Leotti and the Moor were tried by military officers, not for communicating with the "Minnetonka" slaver in the Portuguese schooner of war "Zambesi," but simply for disobedience of orders, and of course acquitted. Leotti had bribed the members of the Court well, and himself and his companion were pronounced innocent of the charge preferred against them.

END OF VOL. I.

R. BORN, PRINTER, GLOUCESTER STREET, REGENT'S PARK.